Technical Analysis Using Multiple Timeframes

****

Understand Market Structure and Profit from Trend Alignment

By Brian Shannon, CMT

LifeVest Publishing, Inc.
Centennial, Colorado

Acknowledgements

A big thank you goes to my editor, Gail Osten. I never appreciated the hard work an editor does until working with Gail. Thanks for all of your great insights, recommendations and making my words so much more readable.

Thanks to those who inspired me to write this book. All the financial authors whose work I have learned from; Jeff Cooper, Stan Weinstein, David Nassar, Larry McMillan, Martin Pring, John Murphy, Fari Hamzei, Michael Covel, Brett Steenbarger, William Jiler, Thomas McCafferty, Mark Fischer, James Cramer, James Altucher, Richard Evans, Toni Turner, Nicholas Darvas, Howard Lindzon, Justin Mamis, John Carter, Timothy Sykes, Martin Schwartz, Andrew Horowitz, Barton Biggs, Roger Lowenstein, W.D.Gann, Gerald Appel, Kira Brecht and many others whose work I have read and learned from over the years.

Thanks to all my fellow blog friends; howardlindzon.com, tradermike.net, thekirkreport.com, bespokeinvest.typepad.com, technologyinvestor.com, ibankcoin.com, bigpicture.typepad.com, thedisciplinedinvestor.com, chrisperruna.com, wallstrip.com, traderfeed.blogspot.com, adamsoptions.blogspot.com, traderjamie.blogspot.com, hamzeianalytics.net, tradinggoddess.blogspot.com, tradingwithtk.com, 1option.com, knighttrader.blogspot.com, maoxian.com, trade-guild.net, timothysykes.com, instantbull.com, fallondpicks.com, uglychart.com, abnormalreturns.com, andyswan.com and many others who I have probably forgotten. You all do great work.

Thanks to Mike Felix and Marco Hidalgo at RealTick.

For the cover art, thanks to Stan Yan of www.squidworks.com/Stan

To all of the viewers of my daily videos at www.alphatrends.net, thank you for all the questions which I hope I have answered.

Thanks to my Mom for her encouragement.

Thanks to my Dad for piquing my interest in the stock market at a young age and for being a great friend.

Thanks to Matthew and Ryan for their confidence, encouragement and patience while I sacrificed too many ski weekends and other quality family time to finish this book.

To the real love of my life, Leanne

And the memory of my brother Eric, you are missed.

CONTENTS

PREFACE

What is your passion? Is there something in life that you think about continually when you are not doing it? Being passionate about something cannot be faked or learned. In fact, it just seems to happen, and it is one of life's rewards that inspire each of us to live life to its fullest.

For many people, passion for life is met through work or sports, and I am fortunate enough to feel a sense of fulfillment from both. It is sad to see someone who does not recognize his or her particular passion, because I believe we are all meant to care about something so much that it becomes a borderline "obsession."

Does the stock market fire a passion in you? Have you ever wished that the weekend would end sooner so you can make a trade you have been planning? Have you ever dreamed about the market? I'll freely admit that I have. It's really not even about the money all the time; to me it is much more related to the mental challenge and the sense of satisfaction that comes from those momentary flashes of market mastery, knowing that I have attained success on my own terms. I do not believe that anyone ever really truly masters the market, but the moments of brilliance and hot streaks that we occasionally achieve more than make up for the periods of mediocrity we experience at times.

No one makes money in the markets all the time. No one! The participants who show consistent out performance are those who understand market structure and respect the always-present risk. Those who are motivated by the love of the game attain a deeper sense of satisfaction from their work than those who are driven solely by the pursuit of wealth.

If you are passionate about the markets, this book will offer you a valuable resource that can be used to further develop your craving for answers about how to achieve market success. I do not pretend to have all the answers. And frankly, if you *do* find someone who makes such claims, you are likely talking to or reading the words of a liar.

This book has been rattling around in my head for years, and initially I was somewhat reluctant to write it because I am still learning and honing my own methods. It is possible, by the way, that some of the concepts laid forth in this book will evolve over time into something that makes them obsolete. I hope not, but it is a possibility.

I will, however, make one guarantee. This book will not make you successful in the stock market, nor will passion alone. If you are searching for the easy way to riches in the market, shut this book right now and buy the one from the liar. You will very likely fail. You see, you can have the knowledge and work hard, but in the end success comes down to one word -- *discipline.* Just like any goal worth pursuing in life, it takes hard work to succeed at trading. Without the discipline to recognize and control the emotions that creep into your decision making process, all of your hard work will likely be condemned to failure.

Financial markets are auctions driven by the actions of the participants, and to truly understand the markets you need to understand the motivations of those who are involved. *It is the goal of this book to help you understand and recognize market structure; this in turn will help you identify your trading edge regardless of which trading timeframe you find most comfortable.*

Throughout the chapters, you'll see a strong emphasis on understanding *why* certain technical formations repeat themselves. Note right off the bat that it is not enough to simply memorize patterns. Any approach to analysis of the markets is truly an art form, and implementing a trading strategy takes that art to another level. *This book will help you understand how to identify low-risk, high-profit trades, and then manage them with a constant emphasis on risk management.*

All of that being said, if your passion involves the ever-changing markets and if you have the discipline to stay with that passion, you will definitely take away some gems.

INTRODUCTION

I have spent much of my adult life studying the markets by poring over innumerable charts in search of the perfect pattern or indicator. I will never close my mind to attaining that "perfection" in the markets. Deep down I am convinced that perfection, whatever that constitutes, does not exist. *To me, the lowest-stress way to profit in the markets consistently is through trend following.* Trends exist on all timeframes, but it is up to you to decide which timeframe suits your personality best. The analysis techniques explained in this book will allow you to analyze and profit from trends on all timeframes.

The number one job of a trader is that of risk manager. Amateurs take risks that make professionals cringe. The fact is that they, too, were once amateurs. They probably frequently look back upon the risky mistakes they made, brought on by greed, which in the end yielded no more than heart palpitations and a lighter bank account. Because greed is a typical trait of the casual market participant, he or she either ignores or is unaware of the risks being taken until it is too late. This is a key realization with which you'll need to cope with early on.

As a trader trying to time the market, your "job" is clear cut: to sync your decisions with price action. To do that consistently, you need to be able to correctly interpret the "message of the market." The goal is to time the trade so that your account is exposed to minimum financial downside and the greatest potential profit.

To succeed at trading, you need to get in tune with the markets rather than impose your own set of beliefs upon them. When the market does not provide clear direction, the correct interpretation should be to sit on the sidelines and preserve capital until the low-risk opportunities present themselves. It has been said that "knowing *when* to be involved in the markets is just as important as knowing *what* to be in." Repeat this to yourself, over and over again. This mantra should continue to resonate with you as you make your trading decisions going forward.

The longer-term out performance of a trader comes from preservation of capital during times of market uncertainty and then having that capital ready to deploy when the market presents conditions that favor your approach. You need only a handful of strategies to be able to attain consistent trading profits. To have more only confuses the issue. The good news is that with all the different products available to trade and all the various timeframes with which to implement strategies, the market provides even the choosiest of strategies with nearly endless opportunities.

You often hear about the need for an "edge" to succeed in trading. After years of trading I know that my particular edge lies in my ability to clearly and objectively observe market action and then implement trades based on what the market dictates. It is never about imposing my beliefs on the market, but rather listening to that market message and executing trades without ego.

The goal of this book is to bring you a solid understanding of market dynamics so you can develop your own market edge based on a comprehensive understanding of market structure. Any strategy based on a thorough understanding of market tendencies should be able to provide the disciplined trader with profits.

The Big "D". If you think about what can and cannot be directly controlled in the markets, the realization quickly floats to the top. There is very little over which you have an influence except your own actions. It follows then that the most important trait for you to possess is discipline:

- You must be willing to accept full responsibility for all your actions.

- You will never find true satisfaction in trading if you expect perfection and make excuses when perfection inevitably eludes you. Without flexibility of opinion and the expectation that trades will not always work in your favor, rigid-minded individuals often fail in the markets because they cannot admit that it is they, not the market, who are wrong when a position goes against them.

- Being bullish or bearish sounds good on media sound bites, but you cannot afford to cling to your outlook if price action is telling you something different. Successful speculation requires a good dose of cynicism.

- You need a well-thought-out plan which anticipates all potential scenarios to keep you from making impulsive and emotional decisions during market hours. You are being bombarded constantly with new information from peers, television, price action, websites, etc. Trading stocks is a business, and if you want your business to thrive you must have a plan which you execute flawlessly.

- When it comes to trade execution, you need to have an idea of what you think is likely in the market, but also must be prepared to respond to whatever the market "gives" you, regardless of what you thought was the most likely outcome.

Each day you should focus on how you can become a better trader so you can pull more money from the market. Is it going to help you make money if you spend your time reading financial periodicals, watching the business channel or listening to other people's opinions? Probably not. Your time will be better spent listening to the only objective market information there is, and that, plain and simple, is price. My approach is to "listen to the message of the market." The collective reasoning, expectations and hopes for a stock are reflected accurately in the price, so it is price action alone that captures my full attention.

To be successful, you'll need to understand what motivates the majority of participants; this will help you anticipate their actions at the correct time and then institute actions of your own.

The only way I know how to effectively measure the collective market actions of all the participants is with technical analysis. In bull markets we hear that the market climbs "a wall of worry;" in bear markets it slides down a "slope of hope." Technical analysis allows us to objectively apply an indifferent eye to our analysis. The hardest part of success is the actual implementation of our analysis in a disciplined way, regulating our emotions rather than falling victim to them at the hands of a market that does not care about us.

Discipline is the most difficult part of the trading equation because, the hard truth is, when you commit capital to the stock market, you also invest your emotions. Your emotions, left unchecked, can often be the catalyst for some very bad decision-making.

Perhaps the biggest characteristic that separates professionals from amateurs is the ability to be unemotional in their market decisions. A professional prepares for all possible outcomes before entering a trade and, as a result, is never in a position to fall prey to emotional decision-making traps that plague the amateur. How do you treat the market, do you find yourself making emotional decisions in reaction to fundamental or technical events? My hope is that this book will teach you to see the market structure clearly so you can position yourself to anticipate market activity and implement your trades like a professional. Once you have learned to view the market properly, it is your job to supply the discipline to trade according to the plan!

Systems-Based and Discretionary Approaches. First let me state that there are no wrong approaches to the market, only wrong approaches for different personalities. There are two broad approaches taken by technical traders -- systems-based and discretionary trading.

Systems traders attempt to quantify market activity and formulate a rules-based approach that is executed with the assistance of a computer. Long before any system is implemented with actual trading dollars, a system is rigorously back-tested to assure that it can survive and profit in "any" market environment. Systems traders believe that, by allowing the computer to implement the trades (program trading), the emotional responses to the market are eliminated from the decision-making process, which allows for more consistent returns. The largest criticism of systems trading is that many of them do not allow for "unexpected market events." It is a well-known fact that as markets inevitably hiccup at various intervals, even rigorous back-testing may not be enough to keep a previously robust system in tune with the market. *During my years of trading I've learned that the "unexpected" seems to happen on a fairly regular basis in the markets.*

With that thought in mind, there are many trading systems in use, and they can provide a way to trade for those who are adept at programming and trust the markets to their computers.

Personally, systems-based trading does not suit my personality. I choose to approach the market with discretion. Discretionary traders place high confidence in their ability to interpret market action and make slight adjustments to their approach as the market action dictates. I believe the personality of the markets make subtle changes that only an experienced trader can detect, and this can lead to an exploitable edge. I do, however, use computers to help me sift through the endless possibilities supplied by the markets each day, and there are specific things I look for when I decide which stocks to trade (this is the subject of later chapters). When it comes time to choose which stocks to trade, when to trade them and related money management decisions, discretion is allowed in implementing the plan.

Being a good stock picker and a successful trader are separate talents, and they require different skills. You can take a good trader and give him a poor setup, but he will still make money because of his trading skills. Flipping this on its head, you can take an inexperienced trader and give him the best setups, but he will still find a way to lose money because of poorly developed trading skills.

Technical vs. Fundamental Analysis. As this book is about technical trading, there will be very little mention of fundamental analysis. As a trend trader, I strongly believe that "news and surprises follow the direction of the trend." To achieve success in short-term trading of equities, traditional fundamental analysis is not necessary (and sometimes is a detriment) to profitable trades. Do not misinterpret my words -- I *do* believe that fundamentals matter, but they are not useful in making short-term trading decisions. It is important to know when a fundamental event may be due for release because it often becomes a catalyst for price movement. However, objective analysis should be made of the *reaction to the event* rather than the formation of an opinion about the company. The market does not care what you think a stock should do. *Again, only price pays.*

To completely dismiss fundamental analysis is to say that the motivations for a large percentage of market participants do not matter. This close-minded thinking is how technical analysts are often portrayed. I am not here to defend technical analysis. I know it works for me, but only because I use it as a framework for my decision making, not as an inflexible system. I am interested in anything that may serve as a catalyst for price change because understanding human nature leads to unbiased analysis that ultimately should lead to greater profitability.

This brings me back to the psychology of the market. Emotions are the enemy in trading, and as such they should be eliminated (or controlled) from the decision-making process. Naturally, this is easier said than done! Studying price charts is about determining where supply and demand forces come together and provide us with a trading edge. To gauge these dynamics, we need to understand the motivations of the participants whose opinions are acted upon in the markets and thereby force price change.

CHAPTER 1
TECHNICAL ANALYSIS

If you want to succeed at trading, you must have a solid understanding of technical analysis. Why? Because trading and investing successfully is about timing, and technical analysis provides the best timing tools available. The markets speak a language which is written on price charts, and they are the pages of a play book that allow us to visualize the unfolding supply and demand dynamics of the markets.

Technical analysis organizes market data so you can develop a practical approach for finding trading ideas, manage entries and exits, determine position size and, not inconsequentially, manage risk. It is not merely a way to analyze market action as some believe, but can provide a complete basis for all of your trading decisions.

Your goal as a trader is to enter a stock as it shows momentum, either higher or lower, stay in the stock as long as it is moving in the anticipated direction and then, hopefully, cash out for a profit once the momentum ebbs. Proper timing allows you to be involved in stocks that are in motion and in cash during periods of indecision.

You cannot time your financial decisions with fundamental analysis, so forget about price-to-earnings ratios, cash flow and dividends right now if you want to succeed as a *trader*. Technical analysis allows you to *objectively* measure supply and demand at work in the market to gain an edge and then determine what might be next for the short-term trend of the stock.

Swim with the Big Fish

Please understand technical analysis is not about memorizing patterns. It is rather about understanding the motivations of participants so you can anticipate their next moves based on historical cyclical precedents...and then take advantage of that knowledge. *If properly understood, technical analysis can provide you with better market clarity by revealing order among what appears to be nothing more than chaotic trading activity.*

If you have ever watched one of the nature programs on television about how many species of fish hunt, you may have seen the larger fish that create "bait balls" by corralling smaller fish into a tight group. Even aquatic mammals like dolphins use this herding technique because it allows a pod to control a school of fish while individual dolphins take turns swimming through the ball to consume their meal. A stock chart is similar because it allows the collective actions of all market participants to be measured in a concise graphical format. The organization of trading data in a consistent form with technical analysis allows us to apply the same analysis techniques to markets that are unrelated beyond the participants who trade them. When viewed together, the actions of a crowd take form, something that might not be revealed to us if we utilized a more narrowly based analysis method. An example of a narrow based technical view of the markets would be to analyze just a level two screen (Figure 1.2). The level 2 is a useful tool at the right time (which we will discuss in future chapters) but it only represents current levels of liquidity in a market with no consideration of past history to keep the analysis in perspective.

Figure 1.1 The price chart is the basic tool of technical analysis. It allows us to study the collective actions of all market participants. RealTick® graphics used with permission of Townsend Analytics © 1986-2008 Townsend Analytics. All rights reserved.

Random Thoughts on Keeping It Simple: Movement of Capital

The analysis I use to trade is fairly simple, relying primarily on price action because price is the only thing that pays! There is nothing wrong with using indicators and oscillators to supplement time and price, but all oscillators and indicators are derived from time and price, so that makes them less important than the actual source of information. Keep that in mind to simplify things.

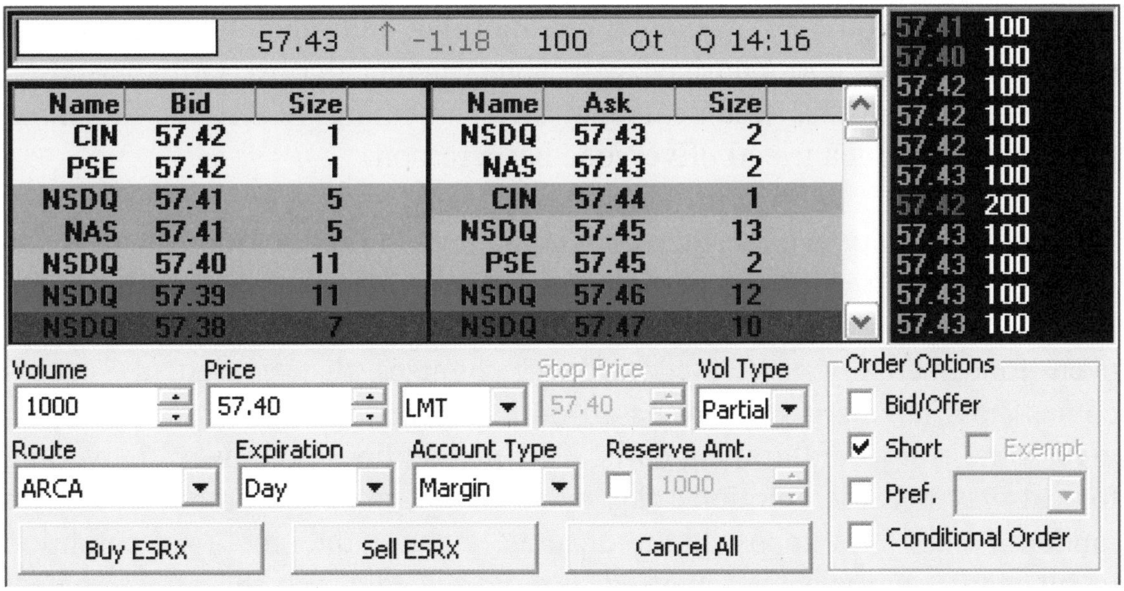

Figure 1.2 The Level 2 screen, which reveals the full depth of the market for a stock, gives us a much narrower glimpse of market action. RealTick by Townsend Analytics.

While it is true that market conditions change, there is an underlying cyclical movement of capital through markets, sectors and individual stocks which, when understood, properly allow us to adapt strategies and methods for profitable trades. A thorough understanding of that market structure allows you to block out the "noise" that elicits emotional responses, which in turn can trip you up and cause losses.

Price charts allow you to separate truth (price) from opinion by focusing on what people are actually doing with their money rather than what they may be saying.

As we'll explore in later chapters, the market is simply a function of supply and demand, with price as the final arbiter. Factors that affect supply and demand vary at different times based on overall risk levels in the market, pending news and other considerations – and individually you and I might not be able to ferret out the extent of their influence on the market. The most accurate way to consistently and objectively observe those forces at work is through technical analysis. The market speaks, and we need to listen. It most certainly doesn't listen to our opinions as much as we would like it to do so.

Incidentally, the market is not as random as some academics would have you believe. Have you ever awakened one morning and randomly purchased a stock? Of course not. You have a reason, whether that reason is based on fundamental analysis, technical analysis, something related to the lunar phase or a tip from a friend. Everyone has a reason.

What defies the logic of academics who believe in random movement is the emotional responses of the participants. Random walkers take a hard line that you simply cannot time the market. But any successful technically or even fundamentally motivated trader recognizes that consistent success comes from having a strategy based on his or her perception of value at a given time, not from throwing darts. The market does not always move in a logical way because emotions play such a large role, and emotions are not random. While it is impossible to accurately gauge the emotional condition of all market participants, charts do provide insight into the psychological make up of the markets. They are extremely eye-opening if we will only let our eyes open to them.

But Does It Work?

The question often asked is: does technical analysis work? As a trader who relies on technical analysis for about 90 percent of my market decisions, you'd expect me to utter an unqualified, "Yes!" It's a bit more complicated than that.

Before deciding whether or not technical analysis "works," we need to pose a more specific question. It is like asking if ice cream tastes good. You may like chocolate but cannot stand the taste of strawberry. So, do you like ice cream? Well, yes and no. I have never done any study of whether a certain pattern "works" or not, but from simple observation and implementation of some of technical concepts, my conclusion is that technical analysis does "work." The market speaks the language of supply and demand, and that message is broadcast on price charts.

We are often asked what "works" in the market -- stochastic, relative strength, MACD, moving averages? The real answer that you will not hear too often is that on a stand-alone basis, none of these tools really work. What *does* work is the disciplined implementation of a well-thought-out plan that is based on an understanding of the psychological motivations of the collective participants.

I realize I've spent a number of paragraphs painting a picture for you, purposely repeating some of the concepts inherent in technical analysis. Now, let me put it in a nutshell:

- It provides us with an overall framework for our price-based analysis.
- As a tool, not a system, it allows us to follow the *flow* of money using price charts to forecast likely future price movements. *The value of technical analysis is not to predict every move but to make sense of price movement.*
- It lets us frame our thoughts and analysis and then formulate a strategy. The market will always provide us with clues as to what is likely to happen. The discipline to follow a plan based on those clues is up to each of us.
- It lends us an unbiased eye that will help us act only when there is a perceived edge. When there is an absence of clarity, the value of the chart is to keep us from making uninformed trades and instead keep our capital safe. The only time professionals place their money at risk is when they have a perceived edge, and if none exists, cash is always the best position.

When you are proficient at recognizing and understanding market structure, it is possible to make a very good living in trading by becoming expert in just a few simple patterns. Yes, just a few simple patterns, uncluttered by a lot of fancy stuff that you don't need. Finding those simple patterns quickly is one way that technical analysis can guide you to market opportunities that make the most sense for your specific criteria.

Looking Forward Versus Just Looking over Your Shoulder
To profit from technical analysis we cannot just look at past history. We have to be forward looking. With past history as our only determinant we are reacting rather than anticipating, and pure anticipators typically profit at the expense of the reactionary participants.

If you anticipate all possible scenarios, it is easier to maintain objectivity and avoid costly emotional decision making. We always have to be prepared for the "what ifs" in trading, or our names will be added to the long list of participants the market has chewed up and spit out. Anyone can recognize an existing trend, but finding the low-risk areas to enter the trend and knowing when to exit is what separates casual observers (sheep) from professionals (wolves). You want to be the wolf.

As a momentum-based trend trader, it is my goal to enter a stock as it begins a renewed trending campaign within a primary trend without exposure to large equity draw downs. To accomplish the dual goals of low risk and high profit potential I always answer these two questions:

1- Where has the stock come from? In other words, where is the potential support for a long trade and resistance for a short trade, the technical levels allow me to determine potential risk and set stops based on objective observation of price.
2- Where does the stock have the potential to go? If my analysis is correct and the stock moves in the anticipated direction, I want to have an approximate price target where the stock has the potential to travel.

When I am satisfied there is sufficient profit potential relative to perceived risks, I buy on strength and sell short on weakness as renewed momentum begins.

Technical analysis can help anyone involved in the markets, from day traders to the longest-term investors. From a technical standpoint, the analysis is the same; it is just the timeframe studied that changes. The price of a security is just as irrelevant as time in measuring the value of technical analysis. The same analysis techniques apply whether a stock trades for $2 or $200 because the participants are the only true market constant, and it is human actions that drive prices.

You have three choices in the markets: you can be long because you expect higher prices; you can be short because you expect prices to decline; or you can keep your assets in cash during times of uncertainty. This material will help you determine when each of those three positions is appropriate at any given time.

Building on Foundations
I suppose a book based on technical analysis would be incomplete if I did not mention the three foundations upon which it is based.

1- **The market is a discounting mechanism**; it discounts the past and anticipates future events. This fact diminishes the value of much of the news on which people base their buy or sell decisions. To profit from market activity, your analysis must be anticipatory rather than reactionary. A strong understanding of market structure allows you to use past history to determine potential future outcomes for a trade.

2- **Prices move in trends**. A trend, once established, is more likely to continue than it is to reverse. That is the basis of trend trading, and much of this book is focused on the identification of and participation in those trends.

3- **History repeats itself.** Perhaps more accurately, as Mark Twain once wrote "history rhymes." The same *exact* pattern rarely shows in the markets. There are many similarities, but few certainties. It is for this reason that your analysis must account for all possible outcomes. If the market does not agree with your analysis, you have a predetermined exit level before a loss is allowed to overwhelm your account.

Remember that this material is designed to provide a method of analysis, not necessarily a trading system. It is up to you to determine how to best use the information based on your personal objectives.

The technical analysis in this book is not based on traditional price patterns such as head and shoulders, triangles, pennants, etc., but rather on the cyclical flow of capital through all asset classes on all timeframes. You will also notice that the charts in this book are all candlestick charts. I use candlestick charts because of their ease of trend recognition and because they are visually pleasing. I do not spend any time on recognition of certain specific candlestick patterns as I have found them to be a distraction to measurement of capital movement across multiple timeframes. I would encourage you to do your own review of candlestick formations to determine if they are useful to you. Never close your mind to new analysis techniques to assist you in understanding market movements.

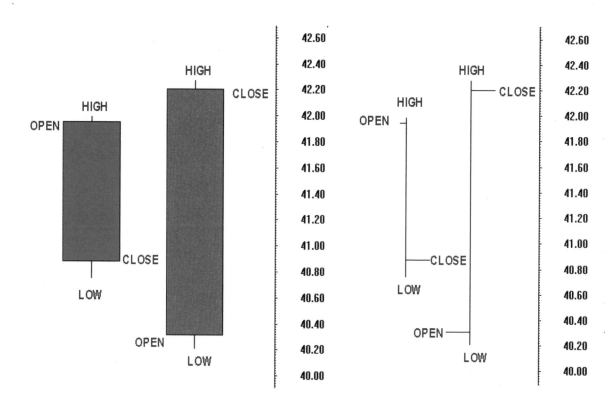

Figure 1.3 The candlestick chart on the left uses color to add another dimension to technical analysis. Red candles represent a period where the closing price is below the open price, while green candles represent a period where prices closed above the opening price. The bar chart on the right displays the open price with a left hash mark and the closing price with the right hash mark. Both forms of analysis show the high and low price for the period of time being studied. RealTick by Townsend Analytics.

CHAPTER 2
THE FOUR STAGES

The market is similar to a living organism. It comes to life each day when the opening bell rings and shuts down after another bell sounds. Like a living being taking a breath, the market continually expands and contracts. The directional expansions in price seek out volume to facilitate trade which, when found, halts price movement and forces price to retreat and recover. This process is repeated countless times as the markets continually seek out the elusive "fair value." The sum of these rallies and declines form an undeniable cyclical pattern that can be found on all timeframes, and understanding this market structure is the subject of the next few chapters.

It is necessary to understand the cyclical flow of capital through all markets before we can get into the study of volume, trends, moving averages and other components on a price chart. All stocks go through their periods during which the public embraces them to times when the participants want absolutely nothing to do with them. There are no good stocks, only good trades, as eventually every "good stock" will become a bad one. A good stock rewards the trader or investor who has correctly positioned himself in the direction of the prevailing trend (either higher or lower). And here's the reality: Because the market is a discounting mechanism, a good stock often has nothing to do with whether the company is considered to be a good one or a bad one when measured with fundamentals. No stock will always behave as expected.

A Stock's Four Stages: Love It, Hate It, Somewhere in Between
Similar to the economic cycle, which consists of: expansion, peak, decline and recovery, stocks can be categorized into four different stages. The concept of stage analysis was popularized by Stan Weinstein in his excellent book, *Secrets for Profiting in Bull and Bear Markets*. For stocks, the four stages are:

1 - Accumulation. Accumulation follows a period of decline; it is the process of buyers fighting for control of the trend. It is a neutral period marked by contraction of price ranges that offer no tradable edge for a trend trader.

2 – Markup. Once buyers have gained control of the stock and a pattern of higher highs and higher lows has been established, the path of least resistance is higher. It is a bull market and traders should be trading the long side aggressively as price expands higher in search of supply.

3 – Distribution. After the market has exhausted the majority of buying demand, sellers become more aggressive, which turns the market neutral. This period of price contraction precedes a decline.

4 – Decline. When the lows of stage 3 are breached, price expands to the downside in search of demand to satisfy the aggressive supply being offered. The pattern of lower highs and lower lows is the hallmark of a bear market, and the only appropriate strategy for a trend trader is to sell short.

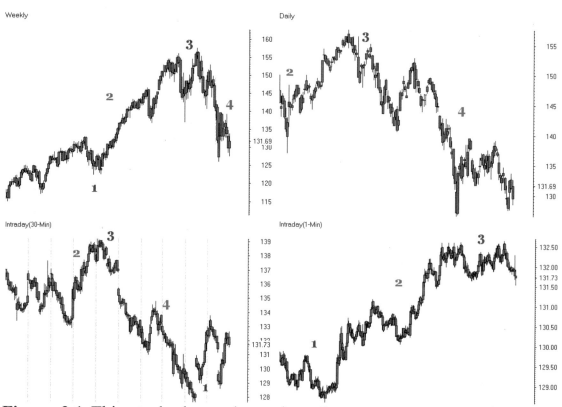

Figure 2.1 This stock shows the various four stages; 1-Accumulation, 2-Markup, 3- Distribution and 4-Decline. The use of multiple timeframes shows how trends can send conflicting messages. RealTick by Townsend Analytics.

These four stages are present on all timeframes and in all stocks. Recognizing them gives you the ability to keep your analysis unbiased and objective regardless of the timeframe you choose, the price of the stock, or trading volume. Fortunately, technical analysis is said to have "fractal" properties. Fractals are defined as "rough geometric shapes which can be subdivided into parts, each of which is approximately a reduced-size copy of the whole." It is not the goal of this book to study fractals to any great degree. However, it is important to know that fractal characteristics show up in technical analysis when we study multiple timeframes. The four stages bring order to stock analysis with the simple assumption that stocks can be trending higher or lower, consolidating, or moving without any clear direction or pattern. Recognition of the cyclical flow of capital throughout all markets is the cornerstone on which I view and trade all markets.

Stocks are similar to different types of athletes with their own unique characteristics and "personalities." Some are "sprinters" who can move very quickly, but tire out and need to rest after a short burst of activity. Other stocks are more like marathon runners who can plod along a course without interruption for much longer periods of time.

One of the basic tools athletes use to monitor their training exertion is a heart rate monitor. The heart rate monitor is useful to both sprinters and endurance athletes as it helps them stay disciplined with their training so they can achieve the maximum benefit without overexerting themselves and burning out. The heart rate monitor for the technical analyst is the price chart. Whether you are someone who is attracted to the fast-moving stocks or the steady "blue chips," technical analysis is a tool that allows you to monitor the actions of all participants, assess risks and determine when to be long, short or in cash.

When I look for stocks to trade I search for the sprinters as they suit my personality best. Investors like Warren Buffet are more interested in the longer-term steady performers. There is not one best way to harvest market profits, just a best way for each individual. You need to figure out which approach is best for you through trial and error.

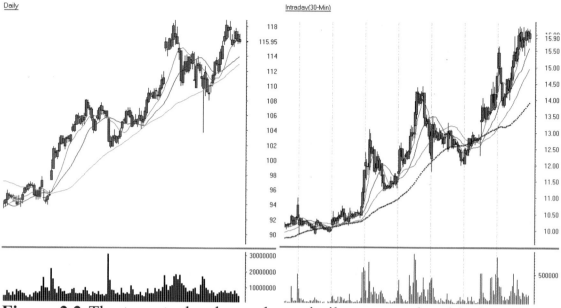

Figure 2.2 The two stocks above show similar up trends with the primary difference being the timeframe. The stock on the left shows a stock in a solid uptrend where the stock gained approximately 25% over the course of 150 days. The stock on the right displays 20 days of data using a 30-minute timeframe and it shows a stock which soared nearly 60%. RealTick by Townsend Analytics.

Stocks alternate betweens periods of trending (expansion of range) activity present in stage 2 and 4, and periods of consolidation (contraction of volatility) during stages 1 and 3. Trend traders always focus on being long the stage 2 stocks and short the stage 4 stocks; they avoid the neutral (stage 1 and 3) stocks. Trending stocks are either moving higher or lower in an easy-to-recognize way. (An uptrend is defined by a series of higher highs and higher lows while a downtrend is defined by a series of lower highs and lower lows.)

In Chapter 10 we will discuss which moving averages best help us to identify in which stage the stock "resides." Generally speaking, in an up trending stock we'll see short-term moving averages above intermediate-term moving averages, which are above longer-term moving averages: all of these averages should have a positive slope to them. Declining markets can be quickly recognized by declining moving averages with the short term below the intermediate term and the intermediate term below the longer-term average. Stocks in stage 1 and stage 3 are transitional and range-bound, with a real battle for control being waged by buyers and sellers. The moving averages in these stocks will be crossing above and below each other, which is interpreted as a lack of consensus of trend.

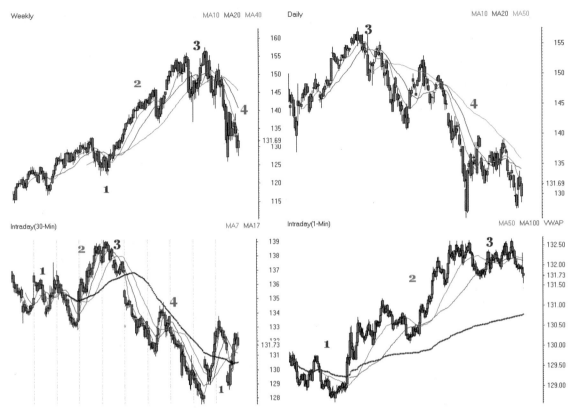

Figure 2.3 This is the same stock in figure 2.1. This time the stock is shown with moving averages overlaid on price. Moving averages offer a reference point to compare price to and help assign further meaning to price. RealTick by Townsend Analytics

A stock in stage 1 or stage 3 is usually correcting after it has experienced a trending move that has temporarily exhausted itself. It's like a runner taking a break. These corrections often occur after a stock has moved to an extreme level due to participation from undisciplined and emotional traders who chase price movement with little regard for risk management. Avoidance of these neutral times allows you to lessen the risk of tying up capital in non-performing assets; you can take advantage of those times to leverage returns by using your money in a trending stock. And if there are no trending opportunities present, a cash position allows time to provide clarity before entering a trade and putting your money back into a risk position.

The short-term consolidation areas within a primary trend are where we want to study price action for clues to a resumption of momentum. In some stocks, it is difficult to identify order on *any* timeframe, and if you are a trend trader, these stocks should be avoided. Trading is challenging enough without getting involved in issues that have a low probability of a successful outcome. *Successful trading is all about finding an edge and exploiting it for your gain. If we cannot find such an advantage, there is no reason to be involved.*

Naturally, regardless of the stage in which a stock resides within the overall cycle, there is always the risk of financial loss, so never let your guard down and become complacent. Losses are possible at any point in the lifecycle of a stock, and your number one job is to guard against those losses.

Emotions and Cyclical Analysis

History repeats itself. The only true constant in the markets is the participants. Humans tend to act, react and overreact in similar ways to certain situations which are repeated over and over again, and this is really the basis on which technical analysis has built its utility. We are merely looking at emotions reflected on a chart to gain insight as to how a crowd may act in a future similar situation.

There are many times when the market appears to be acting "irrationally," and that, unfortunately, becomes the basis for market sheep to impose their beliefs on the market. Those who herd together to question the market typically suffer losses rather than listening objectively to the message of the market and acting accordingly. Don't fall into this trap. As John Maynard Keynes once said, "The markets can remain irrational longer than you can stay solvent." It is said that the collective intelligence of a market sinks to the level of its dumbest participant. That is a scary truth, and it puts an exclamation point on the importance of price action alone.

In trading, emotions are the enemy. You must be able to recognize the enemy and take action to defeat or avoid it, honestly and with introspection, to assess your own strengths and weaknesses all while becoming expert at recognizing crowd behavior. Any time you recognize emotions influencing your market actions you need to take a step back and refocus your attention on price action and the appropriate action dictated by it. Do not allow your emotions to enter the decision-making process. It has been the downfall of many traders.

An understanding of crowd psychology can help you gain an emotional advantage over the average participant who thinks only of his own actions. While we really never know for sure what the feelings and motivations of all the participants are, there are certain emotions which are shared at various stages of a stock's life. Those emotions are represented in Figures 2.4 and 2.5 below. Interestingly, the emotional cycle also has fractal properties. Examine the charts at each level and try to imagine how you would feel – based on the timeframe you use – if you were long or short at each stage.

The range of possible emotions may take an investor several years to experience, or for shorter-term traders, can occur in as little as a day, particularly if leverage is used. Unless you can control emotions from your decision making, leverage is a tool that will magnify those emotions and punish careless trade decisions. If you can recognize the market stages accurately, you can take the appropriate action to minimize the chances of becoming an emotional participant and instead learn to look at the markets with a cold, objective eye. Until you have reached that level of market understanding, you must keep your trading size in check and avoid leverage.

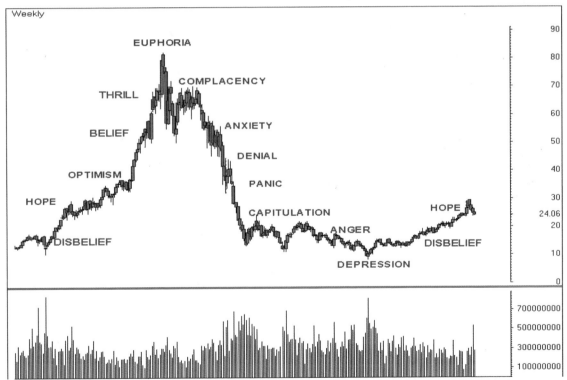

Figure 2.4 Psychology of the long holder at various stages of the cycle.

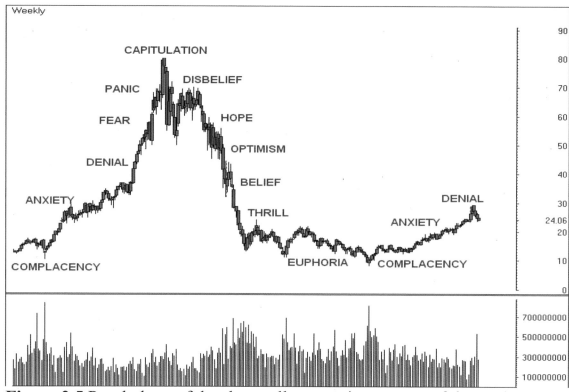

Figure 2.5 Psychology of the short seller at various stages of the cycle.

The charts above are one of an actual stock. The timeframe is unimportant because it could be representative of any stock on any timeframe. These charts are meant to represent the collective psychological makeup of long and short participants in the market during each of the four cyclical stages.

We will study these four stages individually in greater detail in the next few chapters with a continued drumbeat on psychology, since it's the big differentiator between success and failure. In addition, we'll dig into "trend alignment" across multiple timeframes to enhance your odds of finding the lowest-risk, highest-probability trades. Recognition of the stage in which a stock currently resides does not assure that you will make only winning trades. What it does provide is a method for recognizing market structure in order to assign order where others may see chaos. The fact is, there is a lot of random activity in the day-to-day movement of stock prices. The ability to recognize trends and develop strategies to enter and exit trades based on the study of supply and demand can provide you with the edge necessary for consistent profitability.

CHAPTER 3
STAGE 1-ACCUMULATION

In Chapter 2, I outlined the four distinct stages of market activity for stocks, highlighting the characteristics of each. Now we'll take them one at a time, beginning with stage 1 – the accumulation stage.

Accumulation begins with the completion of a downtrend and is a transitional period where the once-aggressive sellers begin to ease their activities. Short sellers realize some of their profits, and sidelined cash is slowly attracted to a perception of value. During accumulation, there is a gradual shift in control from sellers to a more neutral environment. From a momentum point of view, stage one represents a period of diminished volatility and trading volume, as the lack of trend encourages money to seek returns in better-performing stocks. The biggest risk in owning stocks in this stage is time, or opportunity cost, as your money is better deployed in a trending stock.

The tightening of range and loss of interest in a stage one stock is similar to the way in which a bouncing ball loses energy. Think about a ball being dropped from the fifteenth story of a building, with the initial bounce taking it back up to the twelfth story before it drops back to earth. The next time the ball hits the pavement, more energy is absorbed and the ball will not bounce as high as it previously did. The decreased energy in the bouncing ball is similar to how traders lose interest in a stock where the energy is diminished and directional movement wanes. The first few bounces are scary to the long holders, and they quickly exit the stock until all but the most stubborn holders – those with emotions ranging from complacency to denial – are left with positions in the stock.

Eventually the stock loses participants as the longs migrate to other trending stocks, and the bounces are no longer present. The decline, the scary part, ends (stage 4) as the boring stage 1 begins.

Stage one is a period of recovery for a stock, sometimes taking years to redevelop on longer-term timeframes. Even the shorter-term timeframe accumulative action can needlessly tie up capital and should be avoided by trend traders. The old saying, "If they don't scare you out, they will wear you out," refers to the long, tedious process of longer-term buyers and sellers battling for control after a significant decline. Picture a losing football team announcing, "This will be a rebuilding year." That rebuilding year may span several years, of course.

Stage 1: What It Looks Like

Technically, the easiest way to recognize a stock in stage one is a period where moving averages begin to cross above and below each other in a stock where there was a prior downtrend. Near the beginning of stage one, it is common for the longer-term moving average to continue to decline as the healing process for the stock begins. *Moving average crossovers represent indecision, and the accumulative stage is a trendless environment where moving averages will send conflicting messages to those who use them for buy and sell decisions.* The volume will also begin to slow as a more neutral environment is reinforced by price contraction and diminished trading activity.

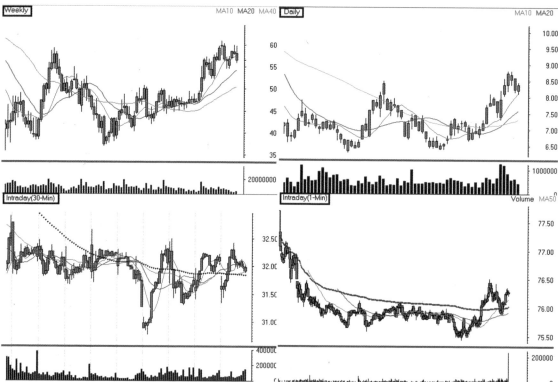

Figure 3.1 Notice the similarities between four different stocks on four different timeframes during the stage 1 accumulation. Moving averages allow us to recognize the prior downtrend followed by trend confusion. RealTick by Townsend Analytics.

Near the beginning of an accumulative phase, there still may be negative news released by the company, but the response from sellers becomes muted as they grow immune to negative fundamental developments, start to ignore past news and become more forward thinking. If you believe that "the bad news comes out at bottoms," as I do, you can also pull your contrarian viewpoint into use and ask, "Well, then who is left to sell?" As a stock begins to neutralize and ranges tighten, the once-present short sellers begin to lose interest in the stock while the long holders become numb to the financial mess they have allowed to take hold in their accounts.

The range-bound activity of a stage 1 stock offers no reason for a trend trader to be involved. There are some traders who prefer the range-bound activity of a stock in the accumulative stage and those traders are content to scalp between the ranges, bidding for shares at the lower end of the range and offering them back out near the upper levels of the range. This "market-maker" approach can be a good low-risk income producer for a patient trader, but there is never a guarantee that the stock will remain confined to a range. Even with what can appear to be a low-risk strategy, it is never acceptable to let your guard down. There are a times where a stock that appears to be undergoing accumulation breaks down further (see Figure 3.2), leaving those who bought before the buyers could establish their dominance with further losses.

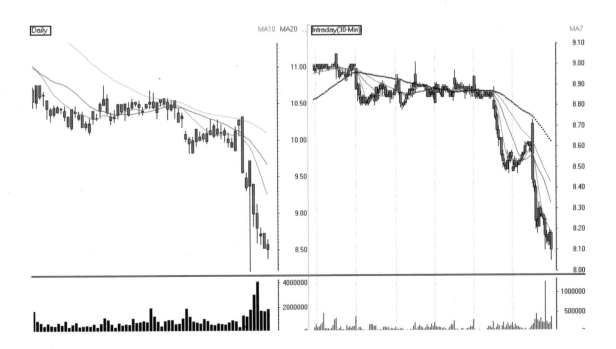

Figure 3.2 The appearance of accumulation is not reason to buy. The longer term selling pressure often continues in a stock which appears to be neutral. RealTick by Townsend Analytics.

While You Sit on the Sidelines, What Are the Institutions Doing?

The ranges from which scalpers attempt to profit are created by the larger forces at work. Large institutional holders of long stock who were unable or unwilling to liquidate their positions in a declining environment will recognize the chances of the stock recovering to previous highs diminishes as time passes and trading volume declines. These institutions often become consistent passive sellers of the stock, which predictably keeps a lid on prices.

On the demand side of the tightening range are the value players who methodically absorb supply and patiently build positions they will stay with for years until the market once again recognizes "value" they perceive to be overlooked. The attempt of the value players is to be the "smart money" group that takes advantage of a stock which was sold off to what they view as a discount to true value.

While a stock in the accumulative phase may bore a trend trader, a large longer-term focused institution welcomes these times because it gives them the opportunity to accumulate a position that will be meaningful to its portfolio. Remember that a large institution does not have the flexibility to enter and exit its full position over a short period in the same way smaller traders do. Buying millions of shares can take months to accomplish unless the institution is willing to sacrifice the quality of execution and drive the share price higher with more hurried purchases.

The quiet accumulation of shares is possible because there typically are no catalysts for movement present. As the stock stabilizes, news from the company often will slow to a trickle as it rebuilds for the future. The lack of activity reinforces the overall diminished volume as buyers and sellers have no compelling reason to act. The lack of confidence from either group brings the stock to a gridlock mired in a mountain of offers and a sea of bids.

There may be occasional glimmers of hope as the company's public relations machines grind out news releases. The release of such news can cause sudden spikes in the stock, but these rallies typically fizzle out until the supply/demand equation has become more favorable to the buyers. *The likelihood of a failed rally increases when the longer-term moving average still exhibits a negative slope to it (see Figure 3.3).*

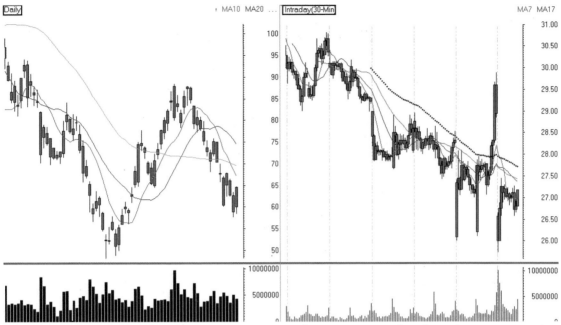

Figure 3.3 While the longer term moving average is showing a negative slope any rally attempt should not be trusted. RealTick by Townsend Analytics.

The accumulation stage is a time of healing for, not just the price of the stock as it stabilizes from the previous damaging sell off, but also for the perception of the stock and even the company. After a large sell off, people who lost money in the stock often feel as though they have been "burned," and depending on the circumstances it can take years for them to trust the auction process in the stock again.

The perception of management of the company may also be tainted by those who lost in the stock. If a stock is down after a period of management mistakes, market participants may be unwilling to commit their capital to the company's stock until there are significant changes in upper management. Do you remember how many of the large bulge bracket brokerage firms ousted executives as the impact of the sub-prime mess caused huge write offs and toppled their stocks? Someone has to take the hit, if only to give investors some vague assurances that the company can move forward once the hurt has subsided. In fact, it is increasingly common for "activist" investors to build large positions in these damaged companies with the intent of owning a large enough position to force management changes.

During the latter stages of accumulation, sellers who are still liquidating long-standing positions become more patient in offering out their shares as they realize their greatly reduced level of inventory is attracting more demand from a larger group of participants. As these longer-term holders begin to recognize that the worst may be behind them, they become less aggressive in offering stock out.

Another scenario which sometimes plays out is that *the institution which had been offering stock out during much of the accumulation period not only stops selling its remaining shares, but starts to repurchase them late in the accumulation.* As crazy as it may sound, a mutual fund may be a net seller one month and a net buyer of the same stock the next month. Unfortunately, mutual funds' decisions to buy and sell are not always motivated solely on making money for their investors. They may still believe in the prospects for a company in the longer term, but because they must disclose their equity holdings at the end of each calendar quarter, they are forced to sell an underperforming stock. The motive is simple: they don't want to look dumb with a large position in a weak stock. The motivation to buy or sell based on how a portfolio looks to the public is know as "window dressing."

Investors in a fund sometimes liquidate their holdings if they believe a manager is not doing a good job. If a fund loses assets due to redemptions, revenues will decrease, bonuses to the manager will decline, or the ultimate firing occurs. Obviously, the manager does not want to deal with these negative consequences; it's easier to just sell an underperforming stock with the intent of repurchasing it when there is less negative feeling toward the company. When the manager senses the stock may be ready to turn higher again, based either on a fundamental development or technical action, he may switch from net seller to net buyer.

A stock can remain in accumulation for years, but when it awakes from its long slumber it can represent an enormous opportunity from the long side. Recognition of the latter stages of accumulation allows not just the institutions, but you, to better anticipate when a new trend may develop. However, be careful. These stocks should not be watched too closely as it will distract your attention from what is actually working today.

Clues to the End of the Accumulation Stage
Some of the first technical clues that a stock is nearing the end of accumulation and readying for a renewed uptrend are *revealed on the chart*

by higher lows, increased trading volume, more frequent tests of a key level of resistance, and the flattening to rising action of longer-term moving averages. (Figure 3.4)

Higher lows are formed in late stage one as diminished supply at lower levels motivates buyers to become more aggressive in their bidding for a stock. The formation of higher lows may also pressure any remaining short sellers to become more proactive buyers than they have been in the past while the stock was dormant. The increasing fear of the short seller is that the stock may be nearing a breakout into an uptrend, causing him to lose significant amounts of money.

The higher lows bring about increased trading volume as competition to own the stock grows. While higher lows may develop, higher highs that would indicate an uptrend are still elusive as a source of supply may continue to offer resistance. When a clear level of established resistance prevents the stock from attaining higher highs, the temporarily insurmountable source of supply becomes challenged more frequently as buyer urgency to own the stock grows. The higher lows create a level of impatience which tempts more buyers into the market. There they can complete their orders by aggressively removing the passive supply which offers the resistance.

As buyers become more aggressive through price (higher lows) and time (resistance is tested more frequently), the stock nears a breakout point. At this stage, the stock also shows the ability to hold above longer-term moving averages, which at this late stage of accumulation should now be turning higher. Thus, this indicates a growing confidence of the longer-term players.

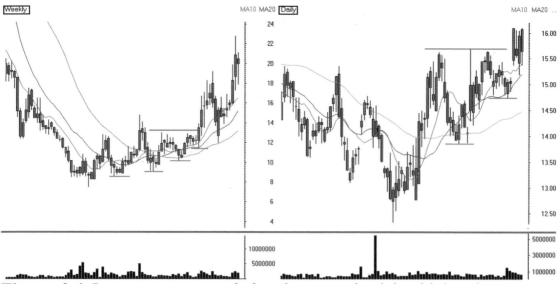

Figure 3.4 Late stage accumulation is recognized by higher lows, more frequent tests of resistance and a flattening to rising of the longer term moving average. RealTick by Townsend Analytics

As the stock nears the breakout point past the resistance level that would form a higher high to complement the higher lows and transition the stock from accumulation to markup, the energy now builds for a breakout. The increased energy is a result of sellers running low on inventory as the longer-term volatility has placed the stock into the hands of "stronger" players.

It is said that the accumulation process moves stock from the hands of weak, uninterested participants to stronger buyers who are interested in holding for longer periods of time based on the belief of a large trend developing. As the stock reaches the breakout point, some larger holders will actually become more aggressive and buy up all the shares available in an attempt to break the stock out of its range and catch other participants off guard. Buying up all of the available shares and forcing a breakout helps bring attention to the stock with news reports of "XYZ was up on large volume to a 20-month high today," etc. These news stories focus more attention on the stock that attracts sidelined cash necessary to sustain a move higher. When the stock breaks above the highs of the accumulation stage and complements the recent higher lows with a higher high, the transition is complete and the stock enters the bullish Stage 2 markup phase.

CHAPTER 4
STAGE 2 MARKUP

The favorite time for the majority of market participants to be involved in the markets is during the bullish stage 2 markup periods. A healthy bull market puts people, even nations, in a good mood as this is when their account values can swell and profits seem to come with ease.

The coveted stage 2 uptrend begins to emerge as the prior accumulation absorbed all significant sources of supply and new buyers compete to own a limited number of shares. *When the stock clears the highs of stage one and establishes a higher high, the buyers are firmly in control of the stock.* With prices above the significant and rising moving averages, the path of least resistance is higher. On a chart, the stock carves out a pattern of higher highs and higher lows, forming what resembles a staircase when viewed from its side. Up, steady, up, steady, up, steady, and so it goes – the "stairway to heaven." Yet within this stage, some "sub-stages" occur, and any technical trader needs to be on the lookout for them before nirvana takes over to an unrealistic degree.

Quite typically, the strong directional move higher will catch a large group of participants off guard and unprepared for the new environment, which then causes them to become emotional, lose discipline and enthusiastically chase prices higher.

The initial move typically is accompanied by some of the largest volume the stock has experienced in months – and the greater the volume, the greater the conviction of the buyers. And the longer it took to complete the preceding accumulation, the greater the pent-up energy and likelihood of continued price appreciation.

Sometimes the initial breakout move is accompanied by good news, but it's not necessary to have a fundamental catalyst for the move to sustain the initial strength. It is possible that the fundamental news may not even be all that appealing this point, but any news looks like good news to the now dominant buyers. Remember that the market is a discounting mechanism and looks forward; news often follows a trend. Learn to trust price, but not completely; that is why stops were designed.

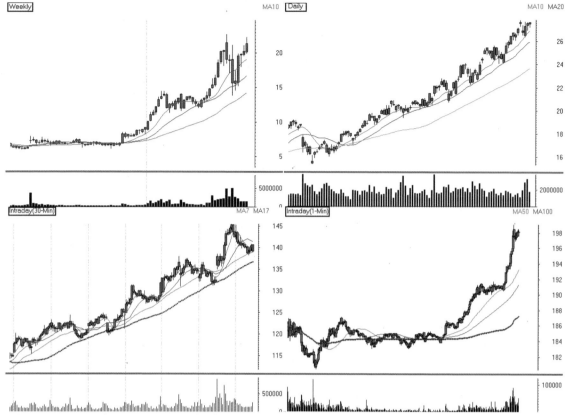

Figure 4.1 The pattern of higher highs and higher lows defines an uptrend on all timeframes. RealTick by Townsend Analytics.

Early in stage 2, the stock's rise will go unchallenged by profit-takers as most longs are "strong holders" who were involved during the long accumulation period. They are not willing to let go of their shares without strong incentives (higher prices). The increased competition to buy the tight supply of stock offered to the market creates an environment in which prices move higher *with ease*. The strong motivation to own the stock early in the trend is intensified by participants from various timeframes eager to latch on to the emerging trend. Short sellers, who failed to cover their positions at lower prices, will create another source of demand as they chase prices higher in an attempt to contain growing losses.

The early moves in an uptrend have a low failure rate. Why? – simply because the supply and demand dynamics – which have set up during stage one and continue with the increased buying pressure from various groups – are quite favorable.

Price: The Motivator

If you've ever tried to buy a high-demand children's toy during the holidays, you'll be able to relate to the next concept. There will always be a price that motivates a source of supply to enter the market and provide liquidity for the buy orders. When the first meaningful sellers enter a stock that has experienced a large and fast rally, these sellers will offer the source that turns the short-term trend neutral and eventually lower. As this source of supply becomes obvious, with prices no longer moving higher with ease, the most aggressive traders will exit the stock and lock in their quick gains. The profit-takers, along with the inevitable short sellers who are attracted to a stock they has traveled too far and too fast, add further supply to the market.

But what about the buyers? As buyers, positioned for a longer-term hold, begin to sense the short-term slowdown in momentum, they may begin to slow their purchases. The hope, of course, is that they may be able to acquire shares at lower prices from the "fast-money crowd," as that group liquidates their longs.

These short-term shifts in supply and demand are repeated over and over during the life of an uptrending stock. As long as the stock continues to find support at a level higher than the low of the last pullback, the uptrend will remain intact.

The very definition of an uptrend – higher highs and higher lows – tells us that the best opportunities for profits in an uptrend come from trading in the direction of the trend. After all, it's no more than simple math: The sum of the rallies will always be greater than the sum of the declines in a primary uptrend.

There are, by the way, some traders who can make excellent money by shorting the short-term rallies and covering on pullbacks, but their job is not as easy or as financially rewarding as those who embrace the trend and exit when the evidence tells them the trend may be ending. Remember, *a trend once established, is more likely to continue than it is to reverse.*

Sheep, Wolves, Eagles and Hawks

Greed and fear are the two most used words when it comes to investor psychology, and nowhere are they more prevalent than in an uptrending market. From an emotional standpoint, the uptrend is a market atmosphere marked by greed of the long participants who crave greater profits.

Often overlooked in an uptrend is the role of fear. As you will learn in chapter 15 on short squeezes, anyone who's ever sold short a stock that's moving higher begins to fear his equity will be wiped out; this, in turn, motivates him to chase prices higher or theoretically risk unlimited losses.

The fear of missing out on a big move higher is another common mental phenomenon in an uptrend. It encourages undisciplined long traders (the sheep) to "graze" in the market after a meaningful short-term rally, often just as the stock begins to experience a short-term correction. At the crest of the momentum, favorable news stories often are the catalyst, encouraging confidence to soar along with purchases.

It is said that a bull market will bail you out of your mistakes, and if you chase a stock early in the uptrend it is likely that some patience will allow you to make up for your short-term timing errors. For most participants, however, that patience will eventually come back to bite them in the rear. Chasing stock prices higher at the expense of discipline and having the trade work out favorably rewards a negative behavior that can be repeated with less-than-stellar results. Failure to recognize and correct this undisciplined approach can create a feeling of complacency (and eventually numbness) when dumb luck runs out and losses inevitably mount from lack of real trading skill. The market is a cruel master where some of the sharpest minds on the planet (the wolves) are trained to feed off character flaws of weak traders who eventually perish.

Enter the Momentum Traders
When the stock has been in the uptrend and has experienced several pullbacks that are resolved back to the upside, the pricing action brings in a strong participation from momentum traders. Shallow and brief corrections are a sign that there is strong demand, but not many willing suppliers show up as party guests. In addition, offers for the stock are spread across multiple levels with little volume at each price level. Market makers know better than to get in the way of such strong momentum. During these times, those brave (dumb) enough to sell short a stock in the midst of a strong advance must be precise in their timing or have very deep pockets to absorb the losses.

There is a marked difference in the psychology of the amateur and a professional when stocks experience strong momentum rallies. Amateurs can best be characterized as eagles during these periods, soaring through the markets with their own self-confidence in high gear. The professional, however, takes on the traits of a hawk looking for its next prey – that prey being the signs of weakening in a trend. This is not paranoia; rather it is part of the trading plan, which so often can be thrown out the window, or at least become sloppy, when the market is going with you. Today's hawks probably were yesterday's eagles who crashed in flight.

Professional traders always play a strong defensive hand and often will lock in partial profits when the stock displays signs of tiring. And then what? After the stock has experienced a brief profit-taking decline, the professional will look for a re-entry as long as the primary trend remains intact. Consolidations which hold above a rising longer-term moving average will often lead to significant upside moves once buyers regain control of the short-term trend.

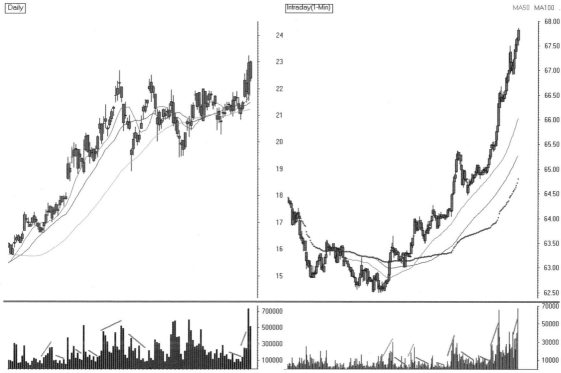

Figure 4.2 The pattern of increasing volume on rallies followed by lighter volume consolidations indicates aggressive buying activity followed by mild profit taking. This pattern reinforces the bullish nature of the uptrend. RealTick by Townsend Analytics.

Studying trading volume allows us to monitor the strength of an uptrend to make sure it's not tiring. *Typically an uptrend can persist when the stock experiences rallies on increasing volume and diminishing volume on the pullbacks.* On the other hand, rallies on *decreasing* volume should be viewed with suspicion, and if volume expands on pullbacks the strength of trend should be questioned.

A stock which shows increased upside velocity will not *always* be accompanied by an expansion of upside volume, however. Much to the frustration of the short sellers, some of the fastest stock movements occur on less volume than previous rallies. The reason the stock is able to continue higher is a simple lack of supply. Short sellers are forced to pay up and buy offers as they panic to limit growing losses. Volume may be light, but only price pays! If you are long, reduce share size and be prepared to exit at the first signs of a weakening trend. Do not become blinded by greed and infatuated with the company or its products and vow to "never sell." Many of the holders who take that oath end up selling much later and at far less favorable prices.

The Broken Stairstep
There is an unrealistic preference among amateurs for a stock that continues higher uninterrupted, while professionals prefer a steady two steps forward one step back type action. Corrections in an uptrend are bullish, normal and necessary for longer-term trends to continue; they provide a natural "cleansing process" where stronger holders accumulate shares from the short-term traders on pullbacks.

A pullback within the trend also gives the early shorts more conviction in their positions, and when they brazenly sell short against the primary uptrend, their sales represent potential future demand.

When the bulls take back control of the market, three things occur:

1 - The stage is set for higher prices as the momentum traders resume their purchases;

2 - Sidelined cash is enticed to buy; and

3 - The short sellers scramble to cover their losing positions.

The longer-term investors are reluctant to offer out stock until after the stock has established higher highs. The picture of increased demand and reduced supply from the strong holders of long positions are the ingredients for higher prices.

When a stock experiences strong upward momentum, it generally is the result of steady institutionally driven buying. Because institutions can have a huge effect on price as their demand for stock pushes prices higher, we'd ideally like to take the ride with them.

It is common for a stock with strong upward momentum to see overwhelmingly positive fundamental developments. Remember, news and surprises tend to follow the direction of the trend. Although there may occasionally be negative news at this point, the stock will often continue higher as short sellers welcome any pullback as an opportunity to trim losses.

You also need to recognize that there can be true surprises which abruptly end the trend. These occurrences are rare, but can be financially and emotionally devastating if quick action to cut losses is ignored in "hopes" that the market over-reacted. As a general guideline, I consider a trend to be broken when it gaps lower by five percent or more (see Figure 4.3). Because this type of price break usually coincides with important fundamental news, be aware of the dates when news is expected for the stocks you trade.

The Late Stage Uptrend: Too Late?
The latter stages of an uptrend are influenced in large part by emotional participants who are attracted to the stock by increasing greed *and* fear. As earlier, fear plays a large role in an uptrend from the short sellers who feel trapped; the buy button is the only relief for trapped short sellers whose losses grow each time the stock ticks higher. Don't make the mistake of selling short if you think the stock is "up too much;" cash is always a better alternative to a short position of a stock in an uptrend.

While it may seem like common sense that the stock cannot continue higher when the momentum expands, the late stage of an uptrend is ruled by emotion, not reason. It is common for late gains to come quickly and travel beyond "reasonable valuations" as optimism builds with late-stage positive news releases. In addition, the role of the early shorts being squeezed creates a buying frenzy. Traditional valuations tools such as P/E ratios are of little value when the patients are seemingly running the asylum.

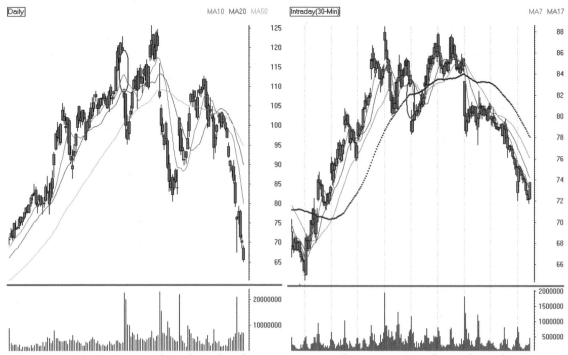

Figure 4.3 Large price breaks in an uptrending stock often foreshadow a stock which will have much greater trouble ahead. RealTick by Townsend Analytics.

In the markets, money goes where it is treated best, and sidelined cash finds its way to the strongest-performing stocks. The lure of easy money from a runaway trend tempts some of the most reluctant buyers of stock to let their guard down and chase the momentum with little regard for risk management. The increased speed of rallies gives the illusion that trading is easy, a situation that is often "relieved" by sudden and sharp bouts of profit taking. *The further a stock travels from a valid level of support the riskier purchases are regardless of how mature the trend.*

In a way, a late stage uptrend becomes a big game of musical chairs. Disciplined momentum traders can thrive in this environment, but it can end badly if a large participant wants to exit the stock quickly, which they often do. Trading the stocks in this part of the uptrend can be dangerous as they can end suddenly.

Evidence of greed-driven fast rallies late in an uptrend should alert you to monitor short-term charts closely because these stocks can decline even quicker than they rallied. Lock in profits before they are taken from you.

It is common for price shocks in this late stage of the uptrend to bounce back, but if the stock is unable to attain a new high quickly, it may be the first signs of a larger source of supply becoming persistent and aggressive.

When sell offs take price down deeper and faster than previous pullbacks, it is a sign of nervousness as traders rush to lock in profits. Large price drops always attract buyers who may eventually regain control of the stock for a while, but it also raises the anxiety of an increasing number of longs. At this point, it will often be the longer-term (advancing) moving averages which attract buying support. When a strong stock does come down quickly, there can be some excellent upside momentum trades, but the large risk of failure must be respected. Otherwise you may quickly find yourself with large losses.

When pullbacks fail to bounce back quickly, it can signal a change in the tone of the auction process, particularly if the sell-off came with increased volume. Sometimes fundamental news events force participants to re-examine their reasons for owning a stock, and as a result, they decide to sell the stock immediately without worrying about the market effect of their selling. When a fundamental catalyst precedes a large and sudden drop in a stock I always sell the stock *immediately* as it often comes towards the end of an uptrend.

When moving averages begin to cross, it is the first sign of trend confusion among different timeframe players. For me that is the beginning of a stock undergoing distribution, and it gives a clear signal that it's time to head onto better trading candidates where a trend is still intact.

CHAPTER 5
STAGE 3 DISTRIBUTION

As with all market cycles, those we'd like to go on forever gradually lose their steam. Bull markets have their day and then eventually sputter. Thus we enter stage 3 distribution. As buyers slowly lose conviction in their purchases and sellers begin to offer more supply, it becomes difficult for the stock to make any further upside progress. The gradual shift from a bullish phase to a neutral environment occurs as short-term traders no longer view the stock as one in which they can attain quick profits. When the fast money crowd realizes the opportunity for short-term upside profits is gone, they sell out and move on to the next hot stock.

The actions of the short-term traders will first decisively show on the charts as the shorter term moving average crosses down through the intermediate term moving average (see Figure 5.1). Just as in the accumulation stage, moving average crossovers represent conflicting trends on the timeframe being studied. *The long-term trend is the sum of the shorter-term trends, and when the moving averages begin to cross, it signals indecision.* The lack of trend agreement indicates different value perceptions by participants operating in different timeframes, and the stock no longer favors high-probability long trades.

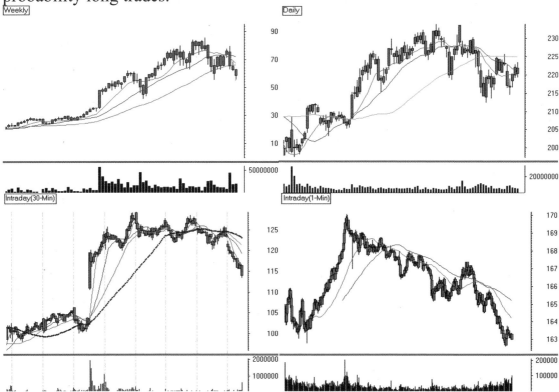

Figure 5.1 Distribution is preceded by an uptrend, it is the gradual shift in control from buyers to sellers. The first signs of distribution on any timeframe are moving average crossovers, where the short term moving average crosses down through a longer term moving average. RealTick by Townsend Analytics.

The Journey from Bullish to Neutral
The beginning stages of distribution often see large volatility as the bulls and bears jockey for control of trend. When this action first reveals itself on the chart, it indicates a transition from a buyer's market to a more neutral environment. As volatility is bled from a previously trending stock, the trend trader needs to drastically reduce expectations for continued upside and search for better trading opportunities.

By the way, *distribution does not assure the stock will reverse to a decline phase, but the indecisive action offers no exploitable edge to traders.* It is possible for the stock to reverse back higher, particularly early on while the longer-term moving average is still advancing (see Figure 5.2). But the more common scenario for a stock experiencing distribution is for a contraction in volatility which offers diminished chances of trending profits.

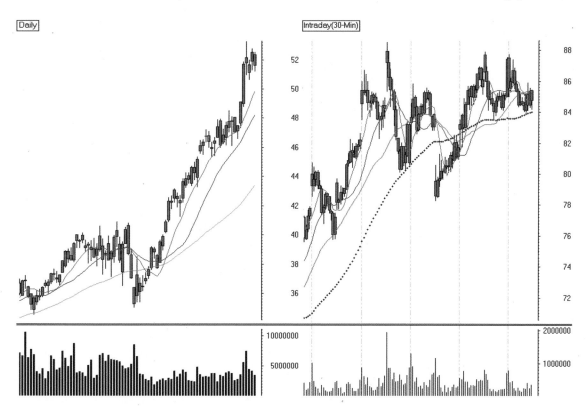

Figure 5.2 The crossing of the short and intermediate term moving averages represents indecision which, when preceded by an advance, should raise our alertness to distribution. What appears to be distribution does not always lead to a breakdown in price. As long as the longer term moving average is rising the benefit of doubt should continue to go to buyers. RealTick by Townsend Analytics.

While aggressive traders can still profit in range-bound markets, a trend trader will find the lack of follow-through momentum to be frustrating. There is no use in tying up capital when there likely are better trend-trading opportunities in other stocks. Frankly, cash is often a better position than experiencing the frustration of trading a stock that stagnates. With cash in hand, you can objectively wait for the right opportunity to redeploy your assets at the right time. When in doubt, stay out!

For many investors, the distribution stage can be a trying time. Positive news stories, stock splits or analyst upgrades are released, and the initial reaction is to jump in. However, these fundamentals mean little as rally attempts are met with supply by the large holders who are paring down their positions; they will *gladly* offer stock to those who buy at this stage. It is common for good news to come out at the top when the stock has already experienced a large rally, so who is left to buy? The process of selling into a news release after the stock has experienced an advance is known as "smart money selling to dumb money."

As the stock is "distributed," trading volume typically is heavier than it had been late in the uptrend as the stock begins to churn. *This big volume without further upside is a classic sign of distribution.*

Remember that the formation of a top in a stock generally takes less time to develop than does a bottom. There are often false moves lower which trap the early short sellers with losses, and when they repurchase those shares it reinforces the neutral nature of the stock. This back and forth price action continues until the buyers run out of conviction and/or the cash to purchase more shares.

During the early to mid stage of distribution, the longer-term moving average will continue to rise. The rising moving average indicates longer term buyers may still be present in the stock during the overall indecisiveness. Any apparent price breakdown, while moving averages are still rising, should not be trusted to continue lower. As the distribution chews up more time, the longer term moving average will begin to "flatten out", indicating a neutralization of the longer term trend.

Here are some things that happen during the middle period of distribution:

- Larger holders who have been net sellers get nervous about shedding shares without negatively impacting the price.
- Buyers still present in the stock become less aggressive and start lowering their bids in search of more favorable prices.
- Some previous buyers become net sellers, thus reducing demand and increasing supply simultaneously.
- Large remaining long positions recognize signs of transition and become more aggressive with sales, hitting bids instead of waiting for buyers to take their offers.

As you can see, there are a number of conflicting emotions taking hold, all of which add up to an indecisive market. The combination of an exhaustion of demand and sellers becoming more methodical in their sales creates a fragile environment for the stock as it seemingly teeters on the edge of a breakdown.

While buyers lose interest and sellers become more aggressive, the temptation is to short the stock in anticipation of a breakdown. As tempting is it may be, do not short here; instead wait for sellers to take control before establishing a short position. As the longer-term moving average begins to flatten out -- and maybe even head lower -- it indicates the increased likelihood of a coming significant price breakdown.

The longer it takes for any technical formation to develop, the greater the subsequent move and, in the case of a top, it is said that "the bigger the top, the bigger the drop." The longer term tops trap more long participants with losses when the stock finally breaks down to new lows, which increases the emotional selling pressure. It can also be assumed that short sellers had more time to accumulate a large position during the longer distribution period. When the stock eventually breaks lower, a larger group of long participants will be looking to liquidate, while shorts will defend their position with additional sales.

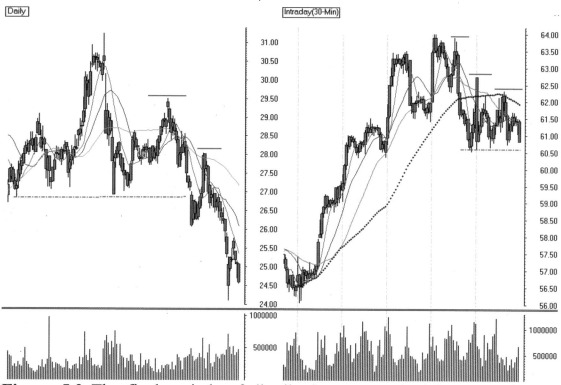

Figure 5.3 The final periods of distribution are marked by; lower highs, flattening to declining longer term moving average, more frequent tests of support and often heavier volume. RealTick by Townsend Analytics.

It's All Downhill Now

As the sellers become more persistent with their supply and as buyer conviction fades, the stock will reveal its weakness on the chart by forming lower highs. An impending breakdown is also shown by the more frequent tests of a support level. The continual absorption of supply at support will weaken the resolve of the buyers and force short sellers to become vicious as they attempt to scare any remaining buyers with their unrelenting sales.

Any bounce from support at this stage is met with supply at a lower level until buyers simply step aside and the stock will experience what is likely to be the first of many fear-driven sell-offs as the stock enters the stage four decline.

CHAPTER 6
STAGE 4 DECLINE

Bear Market! For the majority of market participants, the stage four decline is a dark, scary period that they wish didn't exist. Whether you are a died-in-the-wool bull or someone who feels trapped by the long-only choice of your 401K, a bear market is most participants least favorite time to be involved in the markets. Unfortunately, it is a painful time for many market investors who try to catch a falling knife, rather than wait for it to drop and then pick it up.

For the perennial doomsayers of the world, a bear market is their time to say "I told you so" as they endlessly preach their pessimistic viewpoints.

The fact is, declining equity prices bring about the strongest emotional response -- annoyance from longs to jubilance of the shorts -- from the average participant. However, if you are an objective trader who understands the cyclical nature of the markets, a bear market can represent a terrific opportunity for your short-term profits. Whether you choose to profit from a decline by selling short or simply wish to avoid the carnage to your long exposure, recognition of a bearish environment is essential to the defensive nature of long-term market prosperity.

There have been many attempts to classify exactly what constitutes a bear market, but it simply boils down to this: It is an environment where the path of least resistance is lower for the market being studied. *The sellers are clearly in control and are able to create a condition where lower highs and lower lows prevail. The supply of stock offered to the market is greater than the demand can absorb at current prices, which forces a move lower in search of liquidity.* That's it.

The stage three distributive action which precedes a downturn robs the market of further upside as sellers gradually wrestle control from buyers. When prices break below the lows of stage three and establish the first evidence of lower lows and lower highs a new downtrend has begun and ensuing rallies should be treated as "guilty until proven innocent."

Note that trend reversals *can* occur early on. However, as more long participants are trapped with losses, fear-driven liquidation is more likely and typically will play out in multiple waves. Not only is there an absence of buyers; there is also an increasingly aggressive source of supply from short sellers who apply further pressure to the market. The obvious resulting technical signs of a bearish environment take the stage -- lower lows which form below declining longer-term moving averages.

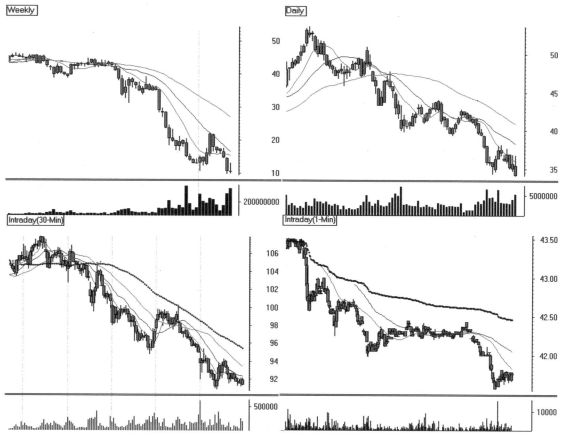

Figure 6.1 The stage 4 decline is marked by lower lows and lower highs. Notice the direction of the moving averages, they can be used to quickly identify "the path of least resistance". RealTick by Townsend Analytics

It is easy and tempting to look at bounces in a primary downtrend and think there is an opportunity to make money from the long side, but simple math favors trading the short side. For example, when a stock drops three points, the only way it can remain in a downtrend is to rally less than three points as a counter trend rally ensues. In other words, *the sum of the declines will always be greater than the sum of the rallies in a downtrend.* Understanding the basis of trend trading (once a trend has been established, the more likely it is to continue than to reverse) increases the likelihood of further downside, and the declines will travel further than the corrective rallies within the downtrend. This creates a powerful reason to embrace short selling.

Short Selling: Powerful, But Handle with Care

OK, the market's headed south. What next? You need to be able to balance your natural sense of hope with the reality of what a chart is objectively telling you and learn to respect the destructive power a downtrend can exert on your equity if you choose to fight the trend. In addition, if you are uncomfortable with selling short, or opposed to it for some personal reason, you will be at a severe disadvantage during a bear market.

Picking bottoms is the hardest job on Wall Street, and frankly, nobody rings a bell at the market bottom. Yet for some reason there seems to be an attraction to declining prices among most participants. Natural human optimism and learned behavior of hunting for bargains in a retail environment provides a "slope of hope" along which stage four stocks decline, crushing the dreams and finances of bewildered longs in its path.

We have all experienced the helpless feeling of searching every news source for a shred of bullishness to justify holding onto a stock in the face of declining prices. This fruitless action only delays the inevitable recognition of truth. It does not erase your losses. It is said that "it is better to be in cash wishing you were in a stock than it is to be in a stock and wishing you were in cash." This is perhaps never truer than the point at which you are "foraging" for a reason to continue on a course that offers little promise.

For long participants, the stage 4 decline is marked by two brands of fear:

- Fear that the stock's descent will continue to wipe out their equity (a good fear to have as it may portend a proper action into cash).
- Fear of feeling stupid for selling "the loser" at a point just before the stock turns higher (a bad fear to have). Do not fall prey to the short-term pauses in a primary downtrend; the short term action will typically be resolved in the direction of the larger, more powerful trend of the longer timeframe.

For short sellers, greed plays a role in a declining stock as they salivate at the increasing equity of their account balances. Short sellers are not immune to fear in a primary downtrend. Short term rallies can come suddenly and quickly in a downtrend and the fear of evaporating profits motivates short sellers to buy. There seems to be a general mistrust of the shorting process and, as such, they are often very quick to cover their positions at the very first sign of any short-term strength.

I tend to be very quick to cover short positions because some of the strongest rallies can occur in a downtrend. Holding a short in the face of such an advance can lead to quick and dramatic losses. I would rather cover my position with a profit and stand aside during short-term, and often violent, rallies and then re-enter the position as the stock begins to weaken again. It is my experience that short-term counter trend moves in a primary downtrend can occur *so* suddenly that trading short is more difficult than long.

Because of the greater volatility in a bear market, shorts generally should be traded more aggressively than longs would be in a bullish environment. When a stock experiences the short-term declines that a short seller targets, there can be terrific opportunities for profits as bids thin out from market makers unwilling to take meaningful inventory and from fearful long holders liquidating in a panic mode.

For a stock in a confirmed downtrend, the rallies are generally feeble, low-volume moves that quickly fail as more frustrated buyers come to the realization that a bottom has not been found. A weak stock is similar to a boxer who continues to stand up to his opponent after repeatedly getting knocked down. The stubborn fighter will ignore the chant of his trainer to "stay down," much the same as buyers keep coming back to the stock hoping to catch the bottom. These participants ignore the shouts of the market to stay away. Yes, the market does "shout" to us, and the screams are represented by the declining moving averages. When a stock experiences a short-term rally, it finds a renewed source of supply at a level which is lower than the last time the sellers took control; this action is represented by the lower highs on the chart. And, of course, a lower low is created as long holders sell out in disgust as they realize they were unable to correctly make their purchases at "the low." See how interconnected this all is?

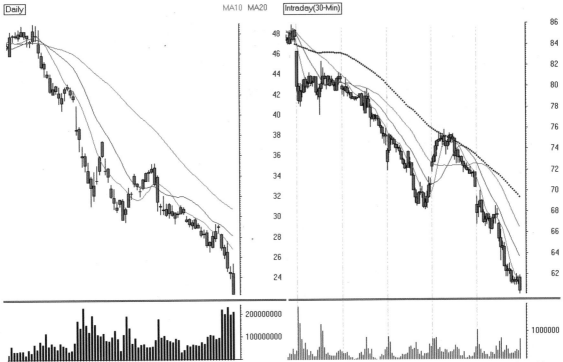

Figure 6.2 Stocks in downtrends can decline very rapidly and their decline leaves broken dreams and account balances for those foolish enough to attempt to pick a bottom. RealTick by Townsend Analytics.

News and Gaps

When a stock has established a series of lower highs and lows, it will sometimes gap higher when there is a news release, analyst upgrade, an announcement of a share repurchase plan by the company, or some other fundamental development.

Understand that sudden rallies in a downtrend can sometimes tempt the most disciplined traders to get long, but it is common for today's hopeful buyers to become tomorrow's fearful sellers as they realize they have been trapped in a stock where sellers have been waiting in the wings for the liquidity to exit.

Do not trust gaps higher in a downtrend, as they have a nasty tendency of reversing. Instead, monitor shorter-term timeframes for opportunities to enter a short as the rally fizzles out.

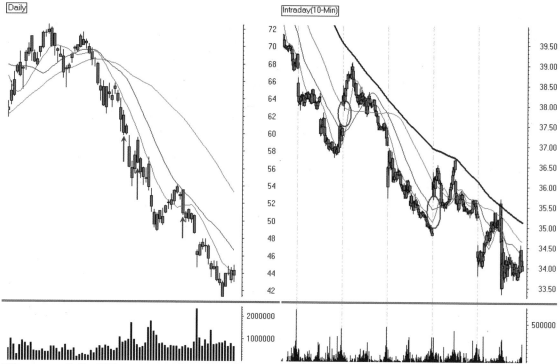

Figure 6.3 When stocks in downtrends gap higher, do not chase the temporary strength which typically fails to hold. Bottoms are a process, not an event. RealTick by Townsend Analytics.

Paradoxically, it is often "bad news" which motivates temporary strength in a declining stock. When a stock has declined for several days without a solid reason and then bad news is released, there often is a knee-jerk sell reaction by the less-informed long holders as they realize the fundamental picture may not be as rosy as their previous research had indicated. When a technically weak stock gaps lower on news, forward-looking short sellers who anticipated it often will take advantage of the liquidity provided by the mini panic and cover some, if not all, of their position.

When bad news brings weak longs to the surface, the stock they sell often is absorbed by better-positioned shorts who are taking partial profits or by stronger buyers attempting to position for a longer-term hold. Larger value players will sometimes begin to initiate long positions when a company reports negative fundamental news, but these purchases are typically just a small piece of a much larger position they will eventually accumulate.

Let me repeat the mantra that using P/E, cash flow and other fundamentals can be harmful as crucial trading determinants in a downward market. During a downtrend, hope tempts market participants to look at these traditional measures of valuation to justify establishing a long position. But only price pays and the message of declining prices says do not buy. In a bearish environment, these valuation tools will drop much lower than most people expect, then revert outside the mean. Price is the only objective measurement of value, and as perceptions change, prices and valuations change.

Another temptation is to get long a declining stock because you feel the stock is "down too much." This thinking is based on the hope that sellers will "come to their senses" and recognize the value. They won't. Logic and reason get thrown out the window when participants act on emotion. Recognize that a stock in a downtrend will bring about those emotions at very inconvenient and financially damaging times for those who were not quick to sell at the first signs of trouble. A stock is never down too much when there is a simple absence of demand.

Is the Decline Nearing an End?
As a stock's decline nears an end, it is common for stronger rallies to develop. These moves higher can be sharp but they typically are short lived as they are driven by short covering rather than true accumulation by longer term holders.

The end of a decline often finds climatic selling action as the last of the stubborn longs liquidate in fear and disgust. Other sidelined participants who have not been involved in the stock may succumb to the temptation of selling short as it becomes "obvious" that the stock is in trouble.

The increased volatility near the end of a decline will begin to taper off as 1) emotional participants get shaken out of their positions and 2) more methodical selling actions of the remaining large positions are gradually overwhelmed by the accumulation of players who are positioning for the next cyclical move higher.

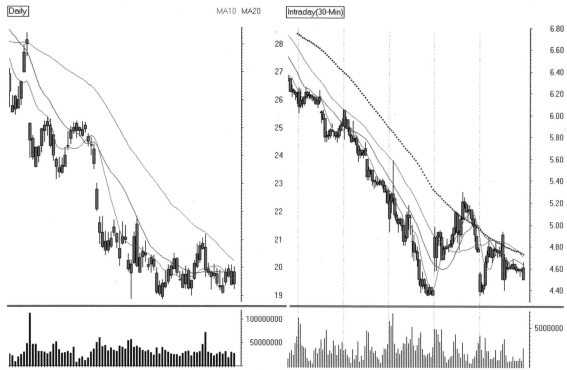

Figure 6.4 Stocks near the end of a stage four decline will often "bounce" higher and encounter further selling near (still declining) longer term moving averages. RealTick by Townsend Analytics.

When a stock begins to show the first signs of higher lows (but not higher highs) it is likely the stock will enter the boring stage 1 accumulation. The end of a decline may be a relief to those who stubbornly stayed long, but that relief is often slowly replaced by a feeling of defeat as the stock turns neutral. As we learned, the accumulation stage can last for years and if they don't scare you out during the decline, they will often wear you out during the accumulation.

CHAPTER 7
SUPPORT & RESISTANCE

Newton's first law of motion states than an object in motion will continue in that direction until it is met with an equal or greater opposite force. One of the greatest mysteries to many participants is how a stock can be in greater demand as prices move higher. Equally as intriguing is why declining prices will force more selling among certain participants.

This confusion is a result of a conditioned perception of "value" that is often based on retail purchases of ordinary goods where a fixed price typically meets predictable demand. In a competitive auction market such as equities, however, prices are in a constant state of flux as they seek the elusive "fair value" in price. Because stock traders' and investors' decisions to buy or sell are influenced by innumerable forces, there exists inelastic supply and demand at varying prices; this results in stock prices that are rarely in a true state of equilibrium.

Elasticity refers to the change in quantity demanded or supplied as prices change. In the case of a price "breakout" past a technical level of resistance, demand typically will swell as supply diminishes. There is a very simple reason for this: sellers realize they are holding a stock where buyers are becoming more aggressive.

This shift in supply and demand causes a stock's price to continue higher in search of an efficient price to satisfy demand. The higher price then induces more supply to enter the market until the amount of shares offered gradually overwhelms the demand. Then prices reverse course.

The everyday reality of these supply and demand factors is far more important than trying to understand every potential reason that could cause participants to change their perception of value. *The levels of consolidation when there is balance in the facilitation of trade are known as support and resistance levels.*

The times when a stock price does meet an "equal and opposite" source of supply or demand results in a temporary unchanged period of time for the price of the stock. These times of horizontal inactivity are the exception to the cyclical movement of prices.

Here's the simplest possible way to think about support and resistance. Throw a ball straight up into the sky. It will continue to rise until gravity overwhelms the force applied to it. For a very brief moment at the top of the arc, the ball will seem to be suspended in the air as it finds "resistance" before falling back to earth. That short period of time when the ball "floats" is very similar to the exact turning point in a stock, the elusive "top" where so many attempt to sell their long position or establish a new short position.

As the ball hurtles back to Earth, the pull of gravity causes it to accelerate right up until the very moment it establishes contact with the ground. The initial violent impact on land is a brief event which absorbs much of the downward energy. The ball momentarily finds "support" and bounces higher again. The time the ball is suspended at the top of its arc or when it establishes contact with Earth is inconsequential to the overall cycle of force, acceleration and gravity.

The same is true for a stock. The time it takes for an exact top or bottom to be established is insignificant, yet it is that fleeting price on which amateurs focus most of their attention.

Making Sense of Directionless Movement
Making money is not about being able to pick tops and bottoms, of course, but rather being involved in an existing trend at a level that exposes you to minimum risk relative to the perceived profit potential. Along the way you will be exposed to periods of directionless movement.

With stocks, the shift in supply and demand can occur rapidly as in the ball example, but it's more likely that there will be a *gradual* transfer of power between bulls and bears. The battle for control of price direction between these two groups forms support and resistance levels, which become the basis for development of trends. These levels are formed as volatility lessens due to a balance between supply and demand, and the market "refreshes" after a strong directional thrust.

The trendless times in a stock's cycle are similar to encountering a traffic circle in a driving situation. You may be speeding along, but as you approach the rotary, you must slow down your car -- perhaps even stop briefly -- if there is a large "supply" of traffic that prevents continued momentum. Your forward movement is halted until enough time has passed to allow other directional movement (cross traffic) to flow. Like a traffic circle, there is no set market clock to indicate when the stock may continue its ascent or decline. In the market, the periods of congestion will simply last until either buyers or sellers regain control of the stock.

For a momentum-oriented trader, directionless movement is a time of uncertainty and not a good time to establish new positions. Longer periods of time and narrowing price ranges allow the stock to build up energy, and this can result in large and fast price movements when the range is broken in either direction. Don't make the mistake of being lured in and caught on the wrong side.

We can never fully understand the exact catalyst that causes market participants to buy or sell at every given time; however greed and fear are at the root of these decisions. All market participants, whether long and short, are motivated by the desire to make more money and are afraid to lose on some level. *Varying levels of fear and greed are what prevent prices from moving in either direction for too long before prices consolidate.*

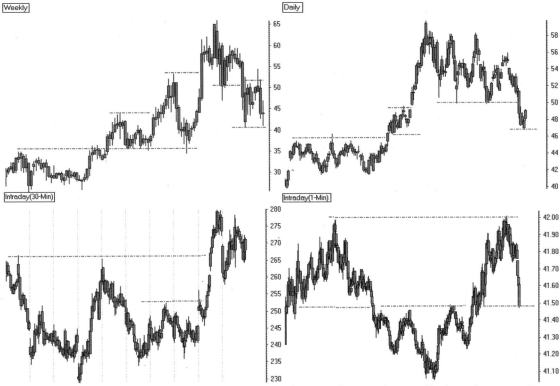

Figure 7.1 Support and resistance levels are formed on all timeframes from weekly charts all the way down to the shortest intraday time intervals. RealTick by Townsend Analytics.

Support and resistance levels are the battlefield where bulls and bears wage their war for control of trend dominance. Generally:

- Resistance levels are formed by passive selling (offering shares vs. selling to the bids) and broken by aggressive buying (buying offers and removing liquidity vs. patiently bidding for shares).
- Support levels are generally formed by passive buying and broken by aggressive selling action.

After any period of price advance, there is always a level at which stocks encounter an equal or greater opposite force that halts their upward momentum. That force is known as resistance and signifies the level at which larger participants perceive that prices have become overvalued. Long holders liquidate positions with a profit (passive fear of giving back gains), and short sellers establish new positions (passive greed anticipating a reversal).

Why Support and Resistance?

A resistance level eventually will signal an ultimate top for a stock, but it is more likely to signal a *temporary level of uncertainty* that then gets resolved back to the upside. When stocks break past levels of resistance, there is often a sudden price surge, which is why many traders pay particular attention to "key" levels of resistance. Resistance levels are broken by fresh money purchases of momentum, short covering to avoid losses, and less supply being offered.

Unless a company goes bankrupt, down-trending stocks will always attract buying at a level of perceived value which halts the decline. Support for a stock is found in an area where buyers begin to meet any source of supply and the stock resists further price decline. Support is formed as short sellers buy back shares sold at higher levels to lock in profits (passive bidding to lock in gains), new buyers who are attracted to what they believe to be bargain prices (passive greed), and a lack of motivated supply (passive fear of selling at the lows). The combination of increased demand and diminished supply makes it difficult for the stock to continue its downward trajectory, as it is supported by demand. When support levels are breached, it can result in a quick move lower as new short positions are established (driven by aggressive greed), long liquidation (driven by aggressive fear of losing) and less demand (passive fear of buying into a decline) coming to a head.

The Memory of the Market

The following is one big psychology lesson, so as you read; let that bubble up into your own psychological approach to the market.

It is said that *price has memory*. It has been shown over and over again that this is not just a convenient saying. However, remember that memory is not just something displayed on a technical chart; it is the shared memory of market participants and how they interact, playing out their psychological games in the market, fear and greed implicit throughout, that is important.

This memory makes it common for a stock to make a return move to a level of prior support or resistance after it has been broken. When resistance levels are broken and the stock experiences an initial surge in price, it is common for the resistance level to be tested on a pullback and hold as support. More simply put, *once broken, support tends to act as resistance* (Figure 7.2). The inverse is also true. *Once broken, resistance tends to act as support* (Figure 7.3).

The key words in those two statements are "tends to act." Nothing is ever certain, so be prepared for those unexpected reversals by using stops to guard against large losses that can result from a failed move.

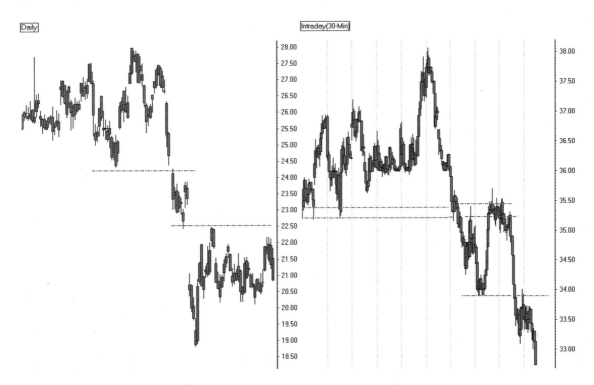

Figure 7.2 Support broken tends to act as resistance as the stock rallies up to the breakdown point. Notice that it is more of an "area" than an exact number where the battles for control of trend are fought. RealTick by Townsend Analytics.

Also note that the breaking of a support or resistance level often is a good place to establish a new position. It is not the breaking of the level that is most important, but the *subsequent action* which confirms or rejects the movement that matters most. Again, have a plan in advance for the moves that fail, an intelligent use of stops can guard against the possibility of larger losses if the move fails.

Figure 7.3 The prior levels of resistance tend to act as support as the stock trends higher. RealTick by Townsend Analytics.

The longer a prior support or resistance level takes to form, the greater the "memory of price" at that level. More participants are validating or assigning meaning to price. Additionally, the more time support and resistance take to form, the more important those levels become to more participants, as these are considered to be "major" support and resistance levels.

The violation of these major consolidation levels causes greater emotional response from participants who are caught off guard and unprepared for the new activity. Beware of the fact that emotional activity tends to create strong momentum moves as careless decisions are made when these unexpected events occur. The less time a support or resistance level takes to form, the less memory is built into price which signifies them as "minor" levels. When minor levels are broken the chances for large momentum development is less likely.

Broken resistance

To understand why resistance broken tends to be support is more important than memorizing a saying. When a range-bound stock clears a resistance area, there often will be a surge in buying as sidelined cash is attracted to the potential of a developing upward move. Short sellers will buy to minimize their losses, and those who previously offered supply also will back off as they realize the stock is in greater demand and the likelihood of more favorable prices may be forthcoming.

When the initial enthusiasm for the breakout encounters a short-term source of supply and then experiences a correction of the upward move, the prior level of resistance will commonly find buyers waiting to become involved.

If the stock has traded below the prior resistance level for a period of time, there will be a large group of participants who "remember" that level as being important. Short sellers who experienced the financial pain of the initial rally will provide support for the stock as they bid for shares to reduce their exposure and limit the accumulation of further losses. Sidelined cash that missed the breakout rally will be attracted to establish new positions near the prior breakout area. On the flip side, short-term profit-takers who drove prices down to the prior resistance level often will discontinue their sales as they recognize the potential for support to be found. As with any turning point in an auction market, it is always an imbalance in supply and demand at perceived levels of value which causes a change in momentum.

Broken support

Just as a broken level of resistance typically acts as support for a stock, a broken level of support tends to act as a level of resistance when the stock returns to the area of the breakdown.

If you consider the actions of longs, shorts and those in cash after a break of support, you will recognize why prior levels of support tend to act as resistance. Have you ever bought a stock just before a sudden decline in price? We all have, and after our initial anger subsides, our next thought is usually, "How am I going to get out of this without a loss?" The buyer's remorse we initially feel leads us to making a vow to get out of the stock if it "just returns to my purchase price."

The longer a stock has held above a key level of support, the more long participants trapped in losses will be looking to sell if prices return to the level from which they broke. When the stock breaks support, short sellers are in a position of strength, and they will defend their short positions by offering out stock near the prior level of support in hopes that their offers will scare weak long holders into selling the stock and creating more weakness from which the shorts will profit. When a stock breaks an important level of support, it is viewed by many participants as damaged goods, and there will be a lack of demand from sidelined cash which exaggerates selling actions and, in turn, weakness in the stock.

It is common for stocks to find support and resistance at price levels where there is reinforced importance placed by technical events such as price gaps, key moving averages, retracement levels, round numbers, prior high volume levels of trading and other technical factors which are less commonly used.

The focus of a trader should not to be to try to buy or sell at a level of support or resistance, but *to determine potential levels* of buying and selling imbalances and use these areas as a catalyst to study price action on shorter timeframes; they then can assess more reasonably if there is, in fact, a momentum slowdown in those areas.

True support and resistance is only known *after* the fact. It is common for amateur technicians to point to a level on the chart where prior important price activity took place and proclaim a support or resistance level. However, in a trending environment those levels will be breached with regularity.

How Strong?
The strength and importance of support and resistance levels is influenced by three factors:
- the time it takes to form
- the volume traded during its formation
- how recently it was developed

The more time it takes to form and the greater the trading volume during the formation of support or resistance, the larger the group of participants whose idea of "value" will be positively or negatively influenced upon a break of that level.

The impact of breaking support or resistance will be magnified when there is a larger group of traders and investors who stand to gain or lose.

And the amount of time since the prior range was formed -- its "freshness" – will determine its relevance to support or resistance levels and how market participants react. Breaks of a fresh range will bring about a greater emotional response from participants. Levels of support or resistance that occurred less recently will not have as much of an impact, as time tends to dull the emotions of participants.

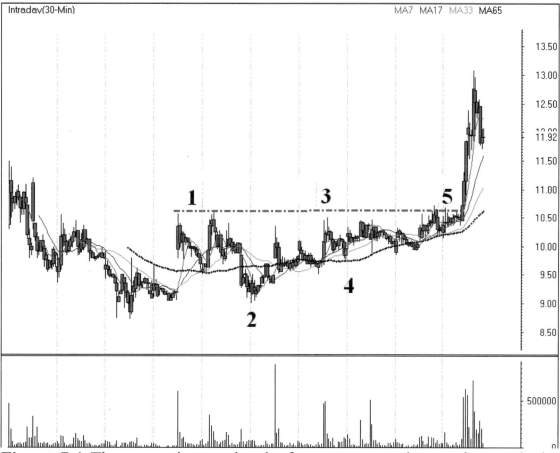

Figure 7.4 The more times a level of support or resistance is tested, the more likely it is for the stock to violate that level. The buyers' increasing frequency in pushing the stock to resistance shows they are becoming more

aggressive time-wise, while the higher lows indicate an increased price aggression. RealTick by Townsend Analytics

The next few paragraphs will refer to the stock in figure 7.4.

1- The above stock repeatedly finds resistance near 10.50. Each successive test of that level removes supply being offered. If there is a seller with 500,000 shares to dispose, the first rally up towards that level may be halted after 300,000 of those shares have been taken before buyers lose conviction.

2- The stock may then pull back slightly to 9.25 before the buyers regain control and are able to push the stock up the 10.50 level again.

3- The second test of resistance may work through an additional 125,000 shares before the stock retreats.

4- Buyers may be more anxious and regain control at a higher level than the last pullback, and the stock may only drop to 9.50 before buyers halt the short-term decline. The ability of buyers to reestablish the upper hand at a higher level shows they are becoming more aggressive through price.

5- With just 75,000 shares remaining of the original 500,000 being offered near 10.50, the next test may be the one where buyers overwhelm the supply and the stock, allowing the stock to break out. These repeated tests of resistance work down the supply in that area and allow the buyers to dominate the auction process.

Figure 7.5 The more times support is tested, the more likely it is that the level will fail to hold the stock up. The lower highs the stock created before the breakdown revealed sellers becoming impatient. RealTick by Townsend Analytics.

Where Is This All Going?

The study of support and resistance levels not only allows us to uncover potential turning points for a stock, but they also help us to objectively determine a potential risk/reward ratio for a stock before we commit capital to a trade. Any time a trade is considered, ask yourself two questions: *where has it come from,* and *where does it have the potential to go?*

Longs should enter just as the stock makes its first higher high on a short-term timeframe. Waiting longer than the initial breakout point to enter puts your equity at greater risk. An initial protective stop should be placed below the most recent higher low, and the further the stock has traveled from that level, the greater risk exposure.

If you find a stock irresistible and think you may be paying more than an ideal level based on the proximity to the actual breakout, use smart money management and trade smaller share size to compensate for the higher risk you are taking.

Determine an upward price objective. What is the likely level where the stock may meet a source of supply that may slow its ascent? If the amount of potential profit is at least three times greater than the level of perceived risk, then the trade setup is worth considering. We will study this further in the chapters on time and risk management.

Support and resistance, once digested, are simple concepts, but understanding the psychology of how these levels are created allows us to better gauge the motivations of the participants so we can clearly see market structure at its purest level.

CHAPTER 8
TRENDS

A trend, once established, is more likely to continue than it is to reverse. That statement is one of the foundations upon which technical analysis is built. For me, it is the best reason for trend trading because trades heading in the direction of the primary trend are where the largest gains will be achieved in any market. I want them.

The direction of the trend is also known as the "path of least resistance" as the stock is able to move largely unchallenged by an offsetting source of supply or demand. The direction of the support and resistance areas, of course, are the pillars on which that trend action is established.

To restate, *an uptrend is marked by a stock that makes higher highs and higher lows* (Figure 8.1), while *a stock in a downtrend makes lower highs and lower lows* (Figure 8.2). What is missing from this definition and needs to be inserted is timeframe. Without any reference to time, trend is ambiguous and can be confusing, as stocks can exhibit up and downtrends simultaneously across varying timeframes.

Figure 8.1 Uptrending stocks move from the "lower left to the upper right" quadrant of a chart. Regardless of the timeframe studied, the action is

defined by higher highs and higher lows. While longer-term moving averages are advancing, the stock should be considered "innocent until proven guilty." RealTick by Townsend Analytics.

If you are a long-term investor, the trends on the monthly and weekly timeframes are most relevant to your analysis, but if you are a day trader your focus is on the trends of the last one to five days. For an investor, a one- to five-day move against the longer-term timeframe is insignificant. A skilled day trader, on the other hand, can earn an exceptional income exploiting those same moves.

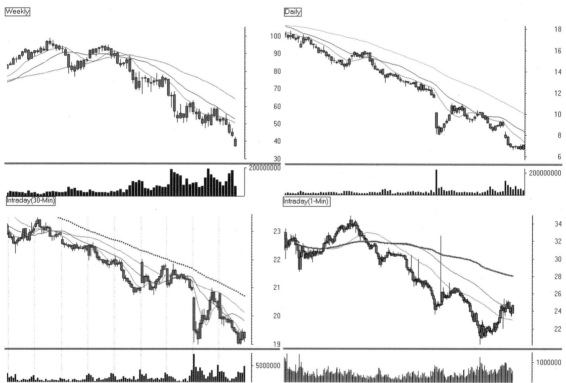

Figure 8.2 Stocks in a downtrend move from the upper left to the lower right quadrant of a chart. The action of a down trending stock is defined by lower highs and lower lows. While longer-term moving averages are declining, the stock should be considered "guilty until proven innocent." RealTick by Townsend Analytics

Alignment across Multiple Timeframes and Consolidation

The highest-probability trades, however, come when there is an alignment of trend across *multiple* timeframes. When there is doubt as to the direction of trend, it is best to refer to the next larger timeframe. Here's why:

- The longer-term more powerful trends exert the most force;
- Short-term corrections occurring in the context of a longer-term timeframe typically will be resolved in the direction of the longer-term timeframe.

My particular bias is that the lowest-risk, highest-probability trades come when you trade in the direction of the *primary trend*. For short-term traders (1-10 days), the primary trend I refer to is found on the daily timeframe.

The reason for trading in the direction of the primary trend is no more than simple math. *In an uptrend, the sum of the rallies will always be greater than the sum of the declines.* Sure, corrections that facilitate short-term profit-taking and some short selling occur along the way, but the odds favor continued upward progress. Obviously, the same principle applies to selling stocks in a downtrend, but in reverse. *The sum of the declines will always be greater than the sum of the rallies in a downtrend.*

In both up trends and downtrends, you *can* profit by trading against the trend, but you will have less opportunity to profit and, frankly, the risks are higher.

The breaking of a longer-term consolidation (stage one accumulation or stage three distribution) attracts players from multiple timeframes (both shorter-term traders and longer-term investors) who attempt to establish new positions near the beginning of a fresh trend. The breaks of consolidation levels from longer-term timeframes tend to lead to sharp and sustained price movement as there is more competition from different timeframe participants for liquidity. As an uptrend unfolds, short sellers scramble to cover their losing positions, sidelined cash is attracted to the momentum, and long holders will be reluctant to offer out their winning positions. As a fresh downtrend develops, long holders make panicked sells, and short sellers recognize the opportunity for profits and offer further supply. Logically, there will be an absence of demand as an attitude of unwillingness to buy "damaged goods" develops.

When a trend begins to develop on a longer-term (monthly or weekly) timeframe, view it as a signal that there will be numerous trading opportunities in coming weeks, months and even years. Once underway, the fresh trend will create alignment trade opportunities after short-term pullbacks. Entries after these pullbacks typically offer a low-risk way to participate in established trends. *The larger the volume on a break of longer consolidation levels, the greater the odds of a new trend being able to sustain the move.* Fundamental developments that accompany a break higher or lower also increase the odds of continued directional movement as more participants are attracted to the action.

And Then There Are the Corrections

All trends experience corrections in their development. Natural profit-taking motivates longs at some point, or it may be another source of supply, often at a prior level of support from a longer-term timeframe; that temporarily interrupts an advance. In a primary downtrend, short sellers succumb to the temptation to lock in their gains as the stock sinks lower and fresh capital becomes attracted to "bargain" prices. These actions create the short-term areas of support and resistance from which trends counter to the primary trend develop. *The counter trend moves are typically resolved in the direction of the longer-term trend.* It takes less energy to continue a trend than it does to reverse one, which is precisely the reason why short-term corrections are most likely to continue in the direction of the dominant trends on the longer-term timeframe.

The tendency for trending stocks is for sudden directional activity followed by a period of digestion for the gain or loss. *In an uptrend, the stock will consolidate the gains, and in a downtrend, the stock price will stabilize after a short-term price shock.* When stocks suddenly surge or decline, it is due to a change in perception as to the value. As we'll cover in Chapter 14 on news, stocks are continually revalued based on perceptions of fundamental *and* technical events. The stock will continue to be revalued in the direction of the primary trend until it meets an equal or opposite force that slows the move. The earlier you are able to recognize the onset of a new trend, the greater the profit potential.

There are two ways that stocks can correct after they experience a surge or drop in price. One is to correct as prices move in the opposite direction of the primary trend, this correction occurs by *price* (known as "pullbacks" in an uptrend and "snapback moves" in a downtrend). The second way for stocks to digest the directional move is through a *time* correction. In a time correction the stock digests the move in a horizontal, low-volatility, trendless manner.

Figure 8.3 This stock shows a correction of the uptrend by a pullback in price. RealTick by Townsend Analytics.

The next several paragraphs examine price movement of the stock in Figure 8.3

1- The first move higher from 65 to 76 took place over two days. It met a source of supply near 76.00 that halted (resisted) the strong upward thrust in price. *Resistance is typically found in an area, rather than at an exact price.* In this case resistance took hold between 73 and 76 before the stock broke lower and sellers temporarily took control. The resistance level was formed near 76 as buyers' actions encountered a heavier source of supply, and upon recognition of the resistance they slowed their buying activities.

2- The initial profit-taking likely caused other traders to lock in some of their gains as the perceived resistance became reinforced with more longs selling.

As it became apparent to sidelined cash that the stock was resisting further upside, short-term short sellers were attracted to the possibility of decline and created further supply by getting short in hopes of the stock breaking lower.

For longer-term long holders, it became apparent that the selling pressure was increasing, and that motivated them to become less aggressive bidders for the stock. They wisely figured that the stock was due to decline further and they could wait for lower prices to make additional purchases. The supply from long profit takers and new short sales combined with decreased demand slowly transitioned the power to the sellers which brought about the inevitable decline in price.

3- As the stock declined down towards 66, further supply was brought onto the market from late profit takers, their actions brought on by a fear of profits slipping away. Momentum short sellers created further supply as the stock declined and bidders, not willing to step in front of the selling, took safety on the sidelines after buying just a few shares.

4- Eventually the stock dropped enough to tempt early short sellers to start taking profits, and their bids helped the stock begin to stabilize. As the new source of demand from short profit-takers works its way to the market, a perceived level of value is established, this attracts other participants to the action. The longer-term longs begin to bid more aggressively for shares; this helps create support for the stock as the final panicky long liquidation is completed.

5- After a day or two of battling for control, the buyers reveal their persistence and begin to get even more aggressive in their purchases by buying up offers rather than waiting for bids to be filled. At the onset of renewed upward momentum, remaining shorts scramble to cover their positions. Short-term trend traders, too, add further demand to the equation as they purchase stock in an attempt to latch onto the emerging strength.

6- With the aggressive sellers flushed from the stock, the buyers' actions have a quick and dramatic effect on price as the stock continues to rally up toward 87 over the next six sessions.

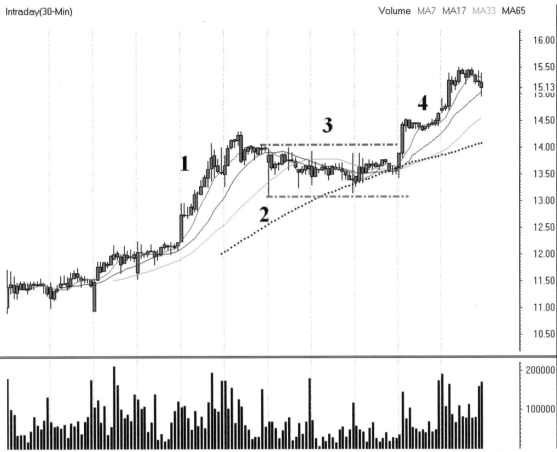

Figure 8.4 This figure illustrates how a stock digests its price gains over time. RealTick by Townsend Analytics

The other way a stock will correct after a directional thrust is to consolidate the gains or losses *over time*. The next several paragraphs reference Figure 8.4 and explain what happens during the course of a time correction.

1- Notice that after a quick run higher from 11.00, buyers encountered a source of supply near 14.00-14.25; this caused them to become a little more cautious and discontinue their aggressive purchases. At the same time, sellers were unwilling to chase the bids much lower.

2- When sellers finally did apply pressure to the stock, bidders waiting near the 13.00 level quickly absorbed the supply. The lack of any steady downward pressure sends a message to buyers that if they are attempting to purchase the stock, they will have to be patient with their bids or chase prices higher. The absence of aggressive selling after a quick run-up in price is a bullish sign as it broadcasts to other participants that the sellers are being patient and anticipating higher prices to liquidate and realize their gains.

3- The more times the stock rallies up to that short-term resistance level of 14.00-14.25, the more likely it is for a breakout to occur as the source of supply in that area diminishes. The longer it takes for the stock to work through the supply, the stronger the holders typically are; unless there is significant upward price movement, they will be unwilling to sell the shares they have accumulated.

When a stock fails to break out quickly, short-term traders get bored and move onto something else. However, the longer-term holders will patiently accumulate shares to sell at a much later date. It is also common for skeptics to sell short the stock in the range thinking that "if it hasn't broken out yet, it's destined to fail." Their selling adds a future source of potential demand.

4- When the stock finally does break past the resistance, short-term trend traders are attracted to the bullish action, and shorts will scramble to cover their losses as quickly as possible. But who will supply these participants with the liquidity for all of that demand? It is likely that a large price movement will occur when this dynamic sets up because the presence of two aggressive sources of demand and one passive source of supply is a combination for quick upward momentum.

Of course, no setup will work out the way we expect all of the time, which is why you can *never* let your guard down. Complacency has no place in trading, so be aware of all possibilities. When a stock does break past resistance, it is expected to continue higher, but failure to do so can result in quick reversals as more long participants become trapped. Learn to recognize this dynamic to avoid being one of the trapped.

Evidence of a Weakening Trend?
Recognition of a new trend is key for finding low risk/ high profit potential trend-trading ideas, but of equal or greater importance is the ability to distinguish clues of a trend that is weakening or about to reverse. One clue that a trend may be losing juice is indicated by weakening volume. Volume measures conviction of the participants, and if volume weakens on successive trending campaigns, it can often signal a trend that's vulnerable to a deeper price correction. Here again, recognize that the only reason to take action of buying or selling comes from price action, volume aberrations are just clues to study price action more closely.

The time it takes for a stock to re-emerge from a correction back into the direction of the primary trend is another indication of lessened conviction from the buyers or sellers. The longer it takes for a move in the direction of the trend of the longer time frame, the less likely it is that the move will continue as a larger battle between bulls and bears is fought.

Trend Lines

Another tool we use for trend measurement is the trend line. The purpose of a trend line is to quantify a trend. Drawing a trend line seems simple enough; you draw a line which connects the higher lows in an uptrend (Figure 8.5) or the lower highs in a downtrend (Figure 8.6). The market does not always make it possible to draw a "perfect" trend line, and there is some degree of subjectivity that comes into drawing one. In practicality, *a trend line is drawn to capture the "essence of the trend," not to confine it to a rigid structure.* One of the smartest things I have heard about trend lines is that they should be drawn with a crayon, not a ruler and pencil. Allowing prices to pass slightly above or below a trend line is often necessary for trend recognition.

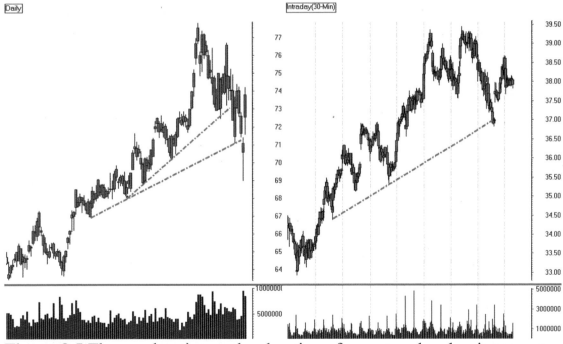

Figure 8.5 The acceleration or deceleration of an uptrend makes it necessary to redraw trend lines. The break of an uptrend line does not assure a new trend lower, only a slowing of upward momentum. RealTick by Townsend Analytics.

Although trend lines often act as support or resistance, *touching a trend line does not give reason to buy or sell*. Instead, it gives us a reason to study the stock on a shorter-term timeframe for a possible low-risk entry when momentum builds back in the direction of the primary trend.

Like any level of support or resistance found in the market, trend lines become weaker each time they are tested. It is common for the fourth test of a trend line to be fatal to a trend. Paradoxically, the longer anything becomes obvious to a large group of participants, the greater the odds of failure.

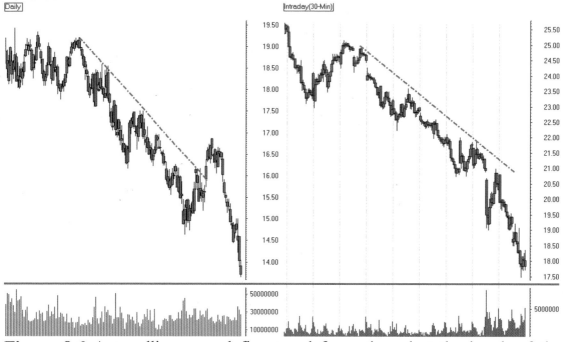

Figure 8.6 A trendline may define trend for a time, but the break of the downtrend line does not always indicate a reversal. RealTick by Townsend Analytics.

Breaking a trend line does sometimes signal the end of the trend; however it does not assure a reversal. When a trend line is broken it should be taken seriously, but it typically signals only that the *rate of change* has slowed, and that the stock is likely to experience a correction through time. This can be an excellent warning of a transition to a more neutral trading environment and the stock should be treated more defensively. There are also many times where a stock may break a trend line, stay below it for a day or two and then continue back in the direction of the primary trend. The moves from a trend line-break reversal can come suddenly, and like any failed move they can provide excellent short-term trading opportunities.

Oddly enough, some of the strongest trending moves develop near the tail end of a trend. A stock which has been trading higher for a long period of time will take on the perception among buyers that the stock is "bulletproof." News typically will be favorable, and a growing reluctance to sell the stock leaves short sellers chasing fewer shares higher as their losses mount. A sharp, late trend move brings inevitable emotion to the stock and *when emotions are high, volatility is generally close by.* As the buyers chase prices ever higher, an unexpected and large source of supply is brought to the market, which can trap the long players like a deer in the headlights. As the selling continues unabated, the bewildered longs become paralyzed with fear as the stock refuses to bounce higher, and losses mount. Without a rally, those long holders will become reluctant sellers as the stock continues lower.

CHAPTER 9
VOLUME

People sometimes question why stock prices change if there is a buyer and seller for every transaction in the market. In a way, that thinking makes sense. Prices change because of an imbalance in supply and demand at a point in time. The market is comprised of countless participants who are all driven to buy and sell by the same motivation, to make money. It is the varying degrees of greed and fear, based on innumerable analysis techniques which stimulate them to act on those emotions at different points in time. As we saw in Chapter 7, supply and demand in competitive markets is inelastic.

It seems counterintuitive to anyone who has bargained on the price of something that your long trade might have a better chance of success if you buy it at a higher price. To understand this concept requires an understanding of how momentum works. If everyone valued stocks in the same way, the agreed-upon price would be a constant, like buying a pair of shoes. When there is the chance of financial gain or loss, the market brings about, and even magnifies, many emotions that do not come into play when buying a pair of shoes. In the markets, it is trading volume that helps us understand the intensity of those emotions.

On a price chart, volume is the first study we add to price. To be clear, volume is added second only to price; it is that important. Trading volume is displayed by vertical bars under the price information directly above. Each volume bar measures the total amount of shares which changed hands for the period of time it took to build the price candle above it.

Understanding how to correctly interpret the price/volume relationship allows us to better gauge the level of commitment of the participants. In a number of ways, volume gives us clues:

- Generally, it assigns meaning to movement that is measured in a more subjective manner than pure dollars and cents.

- It offers insight into market psychology, allowing us to measure the emotional intensity level of the participants in the market being studied.

- It helps determine when there may be the chance for near-term price movement.

- It adds dimension to price study that can be used to confirm price action or signal caution that a move may have difficulty sustaining momentum.

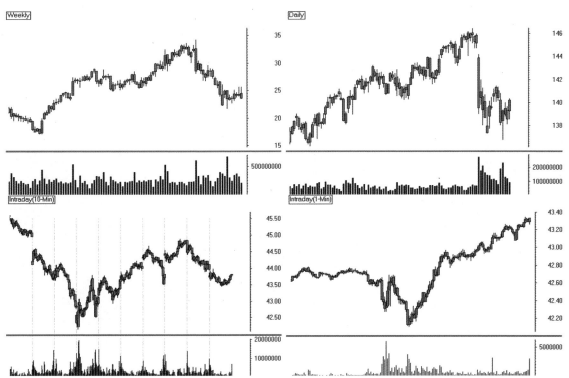

Figure 9.1 Volume is displayed directly below price information. It measures the number of shares traded for the period directly above. RealTick by Townsend Analytics.

The more volume a stock trades, the greater the liquidity (ability to convert to cash), which means that trade is more easily transacted when compared to stocks with lower liquidity. Markets continually seek out volume at each price level and will travel higher or lower in search of an opposite force which satisfies the supply/demand.

Liquidity for stocks is a relative measurement of how many shares change hands. Some stocks trade as little as 50,000 shares per day, while other market favorites trade tens or even hundreds of millions of shares.

An important consideration in measuring liquidity is not just the ease of converting your equities to cash, but what impact your transaction will have on the share price. Market-impact cost can be a negative when it adds unnecessary expense to trading. But it can be a positive, too. There are times when institutions attempt to motivate (manipulate) buyers or sellers by forcing large amounts of supply or demand on a stock. If an institution correctly anticipates the impact of their activities on the market, it can result in continued momentum in the direction of the "manipulation."

Yes, Even *Your* Orders Affect Price
Limit Orders. There are many ways to initiate or dispose of a position in a stock; the two most common methods are either "limit orders" or a "market orders."

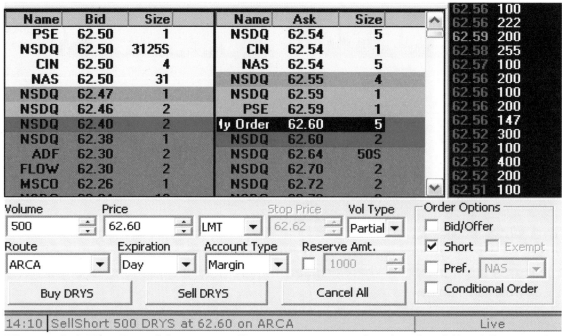

Figure 9.2 The Level 2 screen allows you to see the depth of liquidity on the bid (left) side and the offer (right) side. You can see the highlighted order to sell 500 shares of this stock short at 62.60. This order is a limit order which the market is moving away from as seen by the transaction details on the far right side of the screen. RealTick by Townsend Analytics.

A limit order is one in which you control (put limits on) the price at which your trade will be executed. Consider a stock at a 35.65 bid with a 35.70 offer, and you choose to enter a limit order to buy 1,000 shares at 35.67. When this order is entered, your order will be the best price available to sellers. With this transaction, you are said to be "adding liquidity" to the market because your order adds a new level for prices at which to trade. A limit order is considered to be a "passive" order because there is no direct price movement, as you are waiting for liquidity to come to you. The risk of using a limit order, however, is that no one may be willing to sell the stock to you at the price at which you are bidding. If the market runs higher, your limit order to buy will be left in the dust without having received a fill.

Market Orders. A market order differs from a limit order. Its most important goal is to receive an immediate fill with little concern for price of execution. It is considered to be an aggressive order because it "removes liquidity" from the market. If you were to purchase 1,000 shares of XYX stock at the market, your transaction could potentially have an immediate and substantial impact on price, especially if the quantity of shares you want to buy is more than what is available at one price. If your demand for 1,000 shares is greater than the current amount of supply offered at the quoted offer price, the order would continue to drive prices to a level where your trade is executed.

The appeal of a market order is speed of execution, but the downside is the market impact cost it might cause:

- *For stocks where there exists a deep pool of liquidity (known as "thick stocks"),* a market order for a 1,000-share order will not typically result in adversely affecting the quality of your fill, but a market order for 50,000 shares could have a dramatic and negative affect on the price you receive for the order.

- *Stocks where liquidity is lacking are known as "thin stocks" because few shares trade at each price level.* The use of market orders in a thinly traded stock can be dangerous as your impatience to own the stock may temporarily force prices higher; now you own the stock at an unfavorable price. The extra cost associated with an immediate fill versus waiting for price to come to your limit order is often referred to as "slippage." Smart traders keep slippage to a minimum.

Aggressive/Passive Combos. It is also possible for an order to start out as an aggressive one with the balance being filled passively. Using the same 1,000 shares of XYZ, if you entered a limit order to purchase the stock at

35.70, your purchases would still drive the stock higher, but only to a certain level. With a limit of 35.70, you would be filled on 300 shares at 35.70, and the balance of the order would then become the highest bid at 35.70. Your bid for 700 shares at 35.70 would be the best bid available, but you would become a passive buyer for the balance after aggressively removing supply on the first 300 shares.

The point here is not to teach different types of orders. You probably know those basics already. Instead, I want to illustrate how even a small purchase or sale can affect the price of the stock. The size of the order and number of participants from different timeframes can vary and have a much larger impact on pricing, and that's why volume is such a relevant piece of the market puzzle. It gives an indication as to the level of motivated participants and the urgency of the buyers and sellers. Volume study allows us to glean insights into the emotional intensity level of the participants.

I should also point out that adding or removing liquidity from the markets is rewarded or penalized monetarily by most Electronic Communication Networks (ECNs) such as Archipelago Exchange (ARCA, which was acquired by the New York Stock Exchange). And, by the way, there are now more than 55 equity venues in the U.S., with many dark pools (order books not visible) on the rise. The market is becoming more fragmented both here and abroad.

In order to attract liquidity to their order networks, the ECNs implement pricing costs to remove liquidity and rebates for adding liquidity. As a theoretical example, an ECN may charge $0.005/ share to remove liquidity and provide a rebate of $0.003/share for orders that add liquidity. You can see that the ECN will always come out ahead in this scenario, as liquidity must be removed for any price movement to occur. Some brokerage firms actually charge a flat ECN fee (let's say $0.006/share) regardless of whether the order adds or removes liquidity. When a company charges a fee which may be greater than the actual cost to it, the result is a hidden (and in my opinion, unethical) profit center at the expense of the unknowing customer.

Check your accounts to see that you are not being charged excess ECN fees and getting ripped off. If you enter a large percentage of limit orders, be sure that you receive the rebates. If you ask brokers to credit your account for the rebates, they generally will, but don't expect your phone to ring.

Price and Volume: The Relationship

With an understanding of how our personal trading volume can affect price, let's now look at the larger picture: how to interpret the relationship between price movement and level of trading activity. Proper analysis can confirm or reject the validity of the market's directional bias and identify potential times for expansion or contraction of a trend.

Volume is the best representation of how committed participants are to a market at a given time. Large volume (relative to normal trading activity) can signal times when emotions rule market activity, while low-volume consolidation areas represent complacency. Emotional market activity can be fast and profitable if you possess the proper disciplined mindset to trade it, but it can be a double-edged sword that cuts deeper than the potential reward for undisciplined traders.

In uptrends we witness the greed grow among the longs who are hungry for more profits as their confidence soars. At the same time, fear grips the short sellers who chase prices higher for fear that their equity will be wiped out if the stock continues higher. Their buying can actually exaggerate the upside they are trying to avoid.

The opposite plays out on the short side as long holders are driven by fear of evaporating equity, and the bears salivate at the chance for some quick-kill profits. Their greed escalates as they pile offers onto the stock in an attempt to scare the longs into selling.

Stage 2 Uptrend: What to Look for

Stocks in a stage 2 uptrend exhibit a general pattern of increasing volume as price expands in search of supply and a volume contraction as the stock experiences a short-term correction (either by price or through time). It is considered to be bullish for a stock to move higher on large and increasing volume as it indicates buyers are aggressively purchasing the stock as price moves higher. The relatively lighter and diminishing volume of the pullbacks in an uptrend indicates that sellers are not motivated enough to get out quickly. Instead, the diminished volume of the pullback indicates it will be easier for the buyers to regain the upper hand quickly and that the stock has a good chance of continuing higher. This makes low-volume pullback stocks excellent candidates in which to establish new long positions.

Confirm But Don't Hesitate. Though volume is good confirmation of the conviction of the market participants, don't wait for volume before making your purchases. The only thing that tells us when to buy is price action. If a stock you are watching for potential upside breaks past a level of what appears to be key resistance, it should be purchased as long as the stock is trading at least "normal" volume for the period being studied.

Newer traders often make the mistake of waiting for an increase in volume before they get involved. Unfortunately, the volume they are waiting for to trigger their orders often will come *after* the stock has already experienced a meaningful move. *Volume is used to confirm or reject price direction, not as a timing signal.*

If a stock breaks past a level of resistance and volume is low (relative to recent trading), it should be monitored closely for potential failure. Note, however, that volume often expands with increasing prices as more long participants become confident in their purchases and shorts grow more fearful and chase prices higher. The typical pattern is for trading activity to increase as buyers seek supply, and when the stock encounters a large source of supply the buying activity loses its ability to continue to push the stock price higher. As a stock loses its upward momentum and volume remains heavy, the stock "churns" (meaning heavy trading activity without any directional movement). *Big volume without further upside progress indicates distribution.* If large volume fails to further price movement, the proper course of action is to be on high alert for signs of a coming reversal.

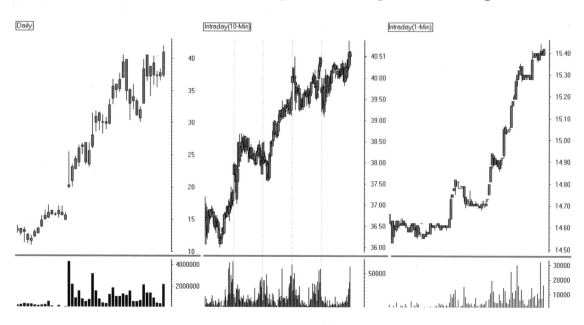

Figure 9.3 Uptrending stocks show a pattern of increased volume as the stock rises, followed by lower-volume consolidations, notice how the heaviest volume tends to be found near the end of a short-term thrust higher. RealTick by Townsend Analytics.

A break of a support or resistance level which is accompanied by a large volume increase often will ignite a move which can be sustained for quite a while. Large increases in volume, after a period of trending activity, often signal that a powerful opposing force has entered the market and the trend may have reached a level of exhaustion. Large volume after a move indicates that emotions are running high among longs and shorts; this usually precedes a turning point in the market.

Even if you are a dyed-in-the-wool technician, it is always prudent to maintain an even higher level of awareness of volume when news is released. News stories often motivate the most emotional participants to enter a stock after a meaningful move has already occurred. Once the "dumbest money" is in the stock, who is left to buy?

When volume patterns fail to confirm price movement they often signal a slowing of momentum or the possibility that a reversal may be at hand. The typical pattern of low-volume pullbacks, relative to the volume on which the stock has advanced, indicates a lack of fear among longs and an underlying strength in the market that leaves the stock in buyers' control. If, instead, the volume of the pullbacks is greater than that on which it rallied, it can indicate large participants are exiting the stock in a hurry because their expectations for continued directional movement are diminished.

When stocks retrace upward movement on increasing volume, they should be exited quickly, and new rally attempts should be viewed with an eye of suspicion. Rallies that occur on decreasing volume should also be treated cautiously; if buyer conviction isn't strong, there is a greater chance of a reversal and loss for the unprepared trader.

Stage 4 Downtrend
Stocks in a stage 4 downtrend exhibit similar volume characteristics as a stock in an uptrend. The similarity lies in the expansion of volume in the direction of the trend and contraction of volume on the counter-trend rallies. The volume in downtrends is often misinterpreted by traders as they see a

stock begin to decline; they fail to exit the position because "it's down on low volume."

Whether a stock declines on low or heavy volume is not the point. When a stock is declining, it is foolish for a trend trader to continue to hold a long position. *Stocks can experience dramatic declines in a period where there is a simple absence of demand and moderate supply.* Stocks decline because there are no buyers, and prices decline to levels that will again attract buying.

A low-volume decline in a stage 2 stock is considered healthy, but when the stock is in a stage 4, it is a dangerous situation for longs who use it as a justification to hold a declining stock. Would you rather lose $10,000 (or any other dollar amount) on heavy volume or on light volume? Seems like a stupid question, right? Losing money stinks regardless of what the volume is telling you, and when prices are moving lower, you should not be holding. Don't fall for reassuring words from an analyst or the CEO of the company. The collective voice of all market participants exiting their positions is the only voice you should listen to, because that *is the market.*

It is quite common for stocks to begin a decline on light volume as the market runs out of buyers and there are only a few sellers present. When prices break, greed begins to boil in the blood of short sellers and fear grows in the longs. As emotions intensify, so too does trading volume. Short sellers sense vulnerability in the longs and will press their bets lower by showing larger offers to the market in hopes of nurturing the fear of the long holders. What began as a low-volume breakdown develops into a more dramatic selling frenzy, and volume really begins to increase. Volume increases in the direction of the primary downtrend as more traders and investors give up their bullish hopes and sell the stock in frustration. When the stock has declined for a period of time, frustration turns into disgust, and a high-volume event (often motivated by news) shakes the last of the stubborn longs out while short sellers rush in to cover their bearish bets. The large volume typically occurs near a turning point for the stock as *big volume without further downside is a sign of accumulation.*

Short-term rallies in a larger stage four decline are typically low-volume events relative to the volume of the most recent selling action. After a stock experiences a quick selloff, it is common for a short-term rally (or bounce) to occur. If the stock is truly weak and the downtrend remains intact, the rally will fall short of the prior rally high, establishing a lower high. The low volume of the rally indicates a lack of motivated buyers as prices have not achieved a level of perceived value to move enough participants to become aggressive buyers and change the trend.

In addition, down-trending stocks that experience a low-volume rally become good candidates for short sales because there remains a high level of anxiety in minds of the recent purchasers and longer-term holders who realize a turnaround may not be happening soon. If the stock rallies on heavier volume than it experienced as it declined, it could signal a change in the direction of trend that should eliminate the stock from short sale consideration.

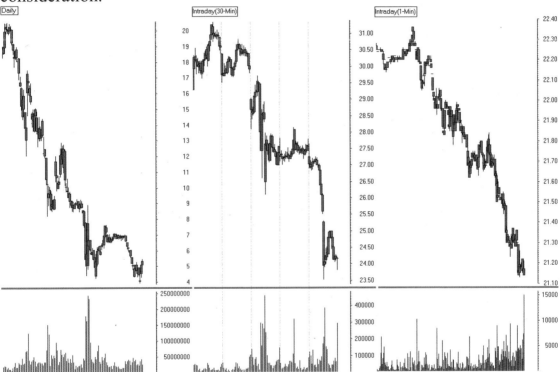

Figure 9.4 A down trending stock shows a pattern of expanding downside volume (which tends to peak near short term lows) followed by lighter volume rallies. RealTick by Townsend Analytics.

Stage 1 and Stage 3
And what of the study of volume patterns in neutral stage 1 or stage 3 stocks? Volume patterns rarely add any value to a trend trader during these stages, but there are some general characteristics of which to be aware.

When stocks experience a period of low volatility, there is little interest in trading the stock, and the low-volume levels simply reinforce the lack of directional price action. The times to be aware of volume in neutral stocks are when there is a large increase in volume as the stock nears an important level of support or resistance. *Unusually large volume often precedes a volatility expansion* and high-volume breaks of support and resistance from low volatility levels typically will lead to a meaningful trending environment. The magnitude of an emerging new trend is magnified by the length of time the stock experienced consolidation. Longer periods of neutrality build more energy, and the larger a move will typically be when the stock breaks out.

Volume: Always Second to Price
Volume analysis can supply us with important information regarding the conviction of the buyers and sellers in a market, but it is important to remember that it comes second to price, as in the end price is the only thing that pays.

There are many instances where a stock will rally on lower-than-average volume, and many participants, afraid a low-volume move will not be sustained, will distrust the move and miss out. Decisions to buy and sell should be based on price action first. If the volume does not expand in the direction of the trend as you would expect, consider reducing your risk by selling off a piece of your position and keeping a tight stop on the balance. Whatever you do, *do not fight a trend because of volume concerns.* Volume will often follow price as more participants are motivated by the emerging trend activity to take action, and fighting the trend can become very costly.

Understand the healthy relationship of the volume expansions in the direction of the primary trend as compared to the diminished volume on the counter-trend moves. This relationship shows conviction in the direction of the primary trend followed by a lack of opposition as the stock consolidates, which increases the likelihood of a trend continuation.

Know that liquidity for a stock is not a constant even when the average daily volume reaches millions of shares. Liquidity is impacted by a long litany of factors such as time of year; time of day; times surrounding corporate events such as earnings, new product developments; and, of course, technical events such as breaking past a key level of support or resistance. Trading volume outside of the normal hours (9:30-4:00 pm EST) tends to be very choppy and is best left to only the most experienced and disciplined traders.

Low-volume times of the year don't necessarily mean avoiding the markets as some believe. One of my favorite times of year to trade is the last two weeks of the year. It seems as though the market becomes more predictable without the influence of the larger program trades. The moves in the more speculative names seem to be left "unchecked" and allowed to run. Be sure to understand the factors that affect the liquidity of the market overall and more importantly, the stocks you are trading, to minimize the impact of your order to the market.

Volume Weighted Average Price (VWAP)

People often wonder why the trading volume slows so dramatically during the middle of each trading day. The most common explanation for the midday inactivity is that it is lunch time. While that is certainly part of the reason, it is not as though the specialists and market makers all head out to a liquid lunch and forget about their business for the day. Most serious traders I know eat lunch at their desks so they don't miss an opportunity and also to maintain a better feel for how their positions are trading.

Consider a market maker with a day order to buy one million shares of a stock for an institutional customer. The market maker cannot buy the full position in the first two hours of the day and then leave his desk to go play golf. Market makers are evaluated by their customers for the quality of trade execution.

The most common method used to analyze the quality of a trade execution is to compare the price the order was filled to the Volume Weighted Average Price (VWAP). The VWAP is calculated by dividing the dollar volume of a stock by the share volume over a given period of time. Simply put, the VWAP is the average price at which each share was executed over the period of time being studied. There are several ways to calculate the VWAP in RealTick, the analysis and trading software I use. I prefer VWAP analysis with a moving average, in particular for shorter-term day trades on a one-day chart of the equity I am trading (see Figure 9.5).

The VWAP is considered to be a fair benchmark for comparison of an institutional trade desk's ability to execute trades on behalf of the customer. If the brokerage purchases are made at a price less than VWAP, the desk is judged to have done a good job for the customer. If the price paid was greater than the VWAP, it may lose that customer. The daily VWAP is a number which changes as orders are transacted at varying prices throughout the day.

Here is a simple example of how an institutional trader might manually execute an order for the purchase of one million shares.

The A.M. Let's say the stock closed on the previous day at $40/share. On the morning the broker receives the buy order; he may *offer* 5,000 or 10,000 shares at 39.90 or lower while simultaneously bidding for shares at a lower price. The first trick the broker may use is to show the full size of the offer while only showing 100 shares bid, in other words, holding a larger number of shares "in reserve." Thus, he really may be bidding for, let's say, 5,000 shares. By showing a larger number of shares for sale and a small amount of demand in the pre-market, the broker may induce weaker holders to sell their shares for fear that there could be a real seller looking to get a head start on their selling that day. This type of activity is pure manipulation, and it happens all the time!

Figure 9.5 The one-minute chart of this stock illustrates an advancing VWAP (represented by the moving average) for most of this day, showing the buyers' dominance. RealTick by Townsend Analytics.

If the buying broker can create a mini-panic on the open, he may be able to scoop up several hundred thousand shares at a very favorable price early on in the day. The risk, of course, is that another buyer could call his bluff and buy the 10,000 shares he is showing the market on the offer. If this does happen, it would put the market maker in a short position of 10,000 shares of a stock for which he has to buy one million shares that day. Either one of these scenarios is possible.

If the market maker is able to secure liquidity for 600,000 shares of the order before noon, he knows his job of filling the balance of the order in the afternoon will be easier, particularly if his 600,000 shares were executed at a favorable price relative to the VWAP at that point of the day. With the majority of the order filled, the market maker can then afford to pull his bids from the market or stop removing supply by taking (buying) offers. The temporary reduction in demand will give the illusion to the market that the buyer may be done and will often cause other (weak) long holders to liquidate their positions; this places further pressure on the supply/demand equation.

With this dynamic of reduced demand taking place, the market maker will still bid for shares, but will lower his bid with more frequency than when he had a larger balance to fill. This action creates more favorable buying conditions and helps the market maker further reduce the average transaction cost for his purchases. This might mean a bigger bonus for him at the end of the month!

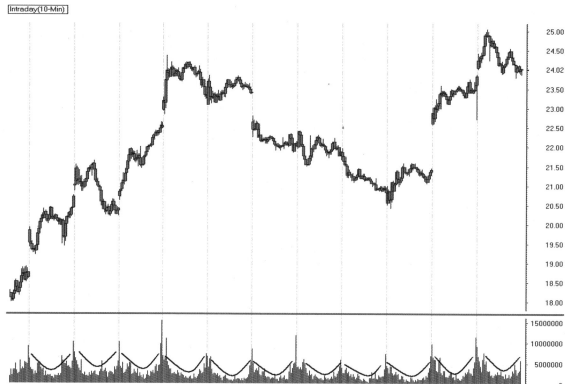

Figure 9.6 The U-shaped volume pattern becomes self-reinforced through the use of VWAP-based execution algorithms. RealTick by Townsend Analytics.

As the Day Wears On. During the midday lower-volume trading, the market maker fills an additional 150,000 shares of the original order, leaving just 250,000 shares to purchase in the afternoon. As the day winds down, the pressure to fill the order in its entirety grows for the executing broker. The market maker may become more aggressive in his purchases because he wants to complete the order. He realizes that, because of favorable prices attained in the morning, he likely will be able to complete the order significantly below the VWAP for the day. This hypothetical scenario is played out every day with many variations by various institutions in countless securities.

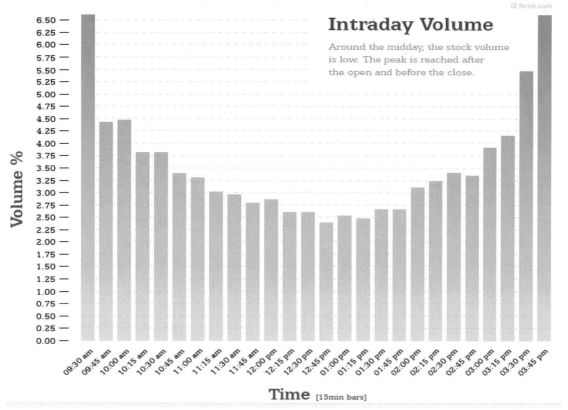

Figure 9.7 This graphic shows the distribution of volume for the S&P 500 stocks at 15-minute intervals over the course of an average day. Chart courtesy of www.finviz.com.

An increasing portion of institutional business today is executed with the assistance of complex algorithms, and a large percentage of algorithmic orders transacted for customers are based on VWAP. Instead of relying solely on talented traders, brokerage firms and, increasingly, their buy-side customers, create execution algorithms in an attempt to attain favorable pricing. The U-shaped volume pattern (Figure 9.7) becomes self-reinforcing by some of these algorithms, as one of the large variables in the algorithmic structure is to execute a certain percentage of volume during the times of day when there is a better chance of receiving a fill with minimal market impact.

Because VWAP is such an important piece of data to the largest market participants, it is something with which every market participant must be familiar with to stay on the correct side of the market.

CHAPTER 10
MOVING AVERAGES

We've already established that after price, volume is the most important study in helping us measure trends. Now let's add moving averages to that study, while not placing *too* much significance to them.

Moving averages are added to the chart to help us assign meaning to price movement by clearly identifying trends. A moving average is simply the average price over a given period of time that changes as older data is replaced with more recent market activity. It is a mathematical trend line which smoothes out the often erratic price data and provides clarity as to who controls the trend for the time being studied.

There are many variations of the moving average, using the high, the low, the midpoint, VWAP or some other variation of calculation. Each of the examples in this book uses moving averages that are calculated based on closing prices. Because we will not be examining the moving averages as a trading system, I find it is irrelevant whether a simple moving average or an exponential moving average is used. There has been much debate about which is superior, but because we'll examine the moving average as a mere reference point to which price is compared -- and not a system -- there is no particular advantage to using one over another.

Simple Math
Calculation of a simple moving average is accomplished by adding up the closing prices for the desired number of days and dividing that sum by the number of data points. To calculate a 5-day moving average, for example, simply add the closing price for the last five days and divide the sum by five. To get the moving property, each new day's close is added to the previous four days and then averaged. With each successive close, the oldest data is dropped off and is replaced by new data to keep the weighting of the average constant.

A simple moving average assigns equal weighting to each data point; in the 5-day moving average, each day's close would have a 20-percent impact on the location of the moving average. Moving averages can be calculated and displayed on any timeframe, from the shortest intraday timeframe chart all the way out to monthly or even yearly timeframes.

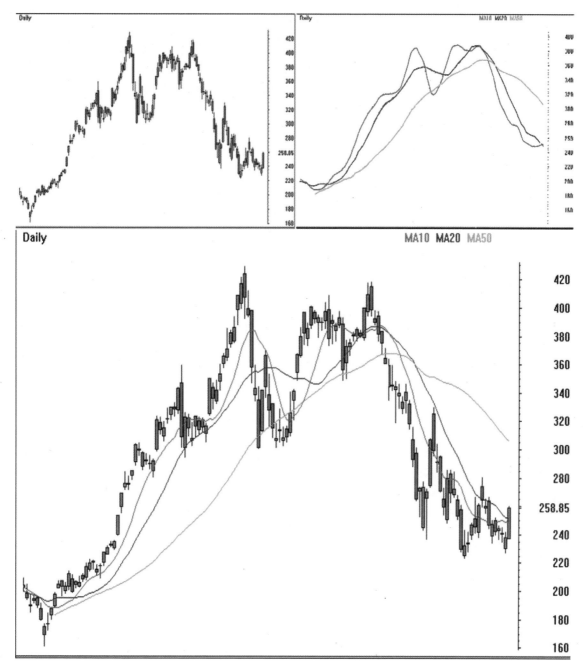

Figure 10.1 The chart in the upper left shows price data alone, while the one in the upper right shows 10-, 20- and 50-day moving averages by themselves. When price and moving averages are combined, it allows for easier trend recognition. The three moving averages approximate a short-, intermediate- and long-term trend for the stock. RealTick by Townsend Analytics.

Because the calculation of moving averages utilizes trade data which has already occurred, they are known as a "lagging indicators." That is often the basis for criticism of their value. The argument is that because they lag price action, moving averages have little predictive power. Frankly, this is a specious argument because our objective is not to use these tools as predictors, but rather as *a visual reference point to which price can be compared in order to better recognize trends and market structure.*

Moving averages are the most commonly found technical indicator on charts because of their simple efficiency in displaying trends. The purpose of a moving average is to smooth out the often volatile and erratic price activity to reduce market "noise" and allow for easy and objective recognition of trends. *In essence, they give us an objective, visual reference point, based on a time constant, to which price is compared.* The use of a time-based constant allows us to more easily spot unusual trading or help determine if the stock is behaving "as it is supposed to."

Moving averages also allow the same analysis techniques to be applied to any market and any timeframe. Note that because there are both minor and major trends on any given timeframe, it is common to use more than one moving average. I prefer to use three different moving averages on each timeframe I study, for short-, intermediate- and long-term trends.

While moving averages are probably the best technical tool to aid us in the recognition of trends, many participants misuse or have too high of an expectation from them. As stated over and over, any buy or sell decision should ultimately be determined by price action. The use of volume and moving averages helps in determinations, but over-reliance on them can choke an otherwise good price action decision.

I also discourage the use of moving averages for systems. Moving average crossovers (where a short-term moving average crosses above or below a longer-term average) are the basis of many systems. *Moving average crossovers are actually a sign of indecision, which is a time to be out of the market, versus trending action which should be acted upon* (Figure 10.2). If your interest is in developing moving average systems, consider adding a break above resistance or below support levels as a further filter.

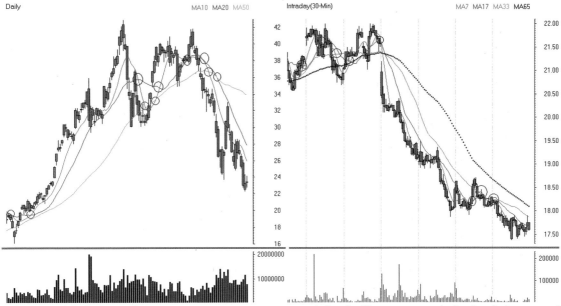

Figure 10.2 Moving average crossovers (circled) represent indecision and are not a good timing tool. RealTick by Townsend Analytics

The Collective Effect of Moving Averages

Because moving averages are so widely watched, their importance takes on added self-reinforcing significance.   Whenever a large enough group of participants believes there is value (or lack of) at a particular level, the collective actions of those participants create the condition believed to exist. The real value of a moving average is the way in which participants respond to price when a key moving average is tested.

For example, the 50-day moving average (Figure 10.3) is a widely watched benchmark of technical valuation by a wide group of traders *and* investors and is thus *often an area that acts as support in an uptrend or as resistance in a downtrend.* You generally can view the action in a stock above a rising 50 DMA as bullish, while a stock below a declining 50 DMA should be considered highly suspect and vulnerable to further decline.   There is no technical analysis voodoo for this tendency.   Rather it becomes important because enough participants *believe* it to be significant, and their buying and selling actions based on that perception cause it to become *a technical inflection point where value is often negotiated.*

When large holders of stock, who have been lightening their position by selling shares in an uptrend, see the stock approaching the 50-day moving average, they will often slow their selling because they have been conditioned to recognize that the rising 50-day MA often acts as support.

The reduced supply from these large long holders helps the 50-day MA regain its footing as less supply is offered.

At the same time that less supply is brought to the market, there is a slow shift in the buy/side dynamics. Short sellers who established positions for a move lower often will begin to bid for the shares back near the 50-day moving average because they have seen it act as support for so many other stocks before. They figure it is a good level at which to reduce their exposure and lock in some profits.

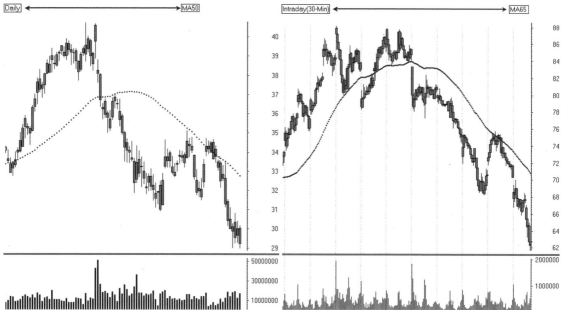

Figure 10.3 The daily chart on the left has a 50-day simple moving average, while the chart with 30-minute data on the right displays a 65-period (the market is open for 6.5 hours per day or 13 30-minute periods; over five days the market is open for 65 30-minute periods) simple moving average. RealTick by Townsend Analytics.

Sidelined cash, too, will be attracted to a stock that has experienced a pullback to a 50-day moving average. Because these traders have seen so many stocks "bounce higher" after testing the average, they begin to establish long positions.

The value of the 50-day moving average to these participants is based on a perception of value in that area, but it is the collective actions of those participants which brings about the shift in supply and demand that may lead to the subsequent move higher. The psychology of other period moving averages we will study is the same. In a way, a moving average sets off a

90

"Pavlovian" response from participants who are conditioned to viewing moving averages as support or resistance.

Timing Tools? Probably Not

By themselves, moving averages are not good timing tools. The proper way for a trader to use moving averages is not to take action based on the average, but to observe the action more closely as price approaches a moving average.

The unfolding action at the 50-day moving average may be the catalyst that draws our attention to study the stock, but action to buy or sell should only come after closer examination of the stock on a shorter-term timeframe. That shorter-term timeframe allows us to hone in our analysis of the battle being waged at the 50- (or any other) day moving average. *The longer-term timeframe action is what draws our attention to the stock, but the low-risk entry comes from a deeper study of the auction process on the shorter-term timeframes.* And only price tells us when to buy or sell, leaving the moving average as a mere inflection point that draws our attention to a price level so we can understand where a potential shift in the supply/demand dynamics is likely to take place.

The Trend is Your Friend

Regardless of which timeframes you choose to trade or study price action, you want to trade the path of least resistance, and the direction of the moving averages allows you to quickly determine that direction. Rising moving averages represent positive price action, while declining moving averages are the result of net selling. Bulls rule the auction process above the long-term moving average for each timeframe (defined in the table below), and the stock should be considered "innocent until proven guilty" as long as the key moving averages are advancing. Bears preside below the declining moving average, and when the longer-term moving average is declining, that stock should also be considered "guilty until proven innocent."

Note that *the direction of key moving averages is more important than a close above or below them* (figure 10.3). It is a common trap for uninformed short sellers to initiate a new position on the first few days of a close below a key moving average, but as long as the moving average is trending higher the benefit of doubt should continue to go to the buyers. Just as common is the tendency for fresh buyers to become excited as a stock crosses above a declining key moving average. These rally attempts will typically fail until the key moving average flattens out or begins to turn higher.

Amateur technicians often analyze moving averages in search of literal entry and exit levels, while more experienced traders study moving averages to help determine the unfolding psychological shifts in market sentiment so they can anticipate a low-risk, high-probability trading scenario. It is one of the market's cruelest tendencies to trap a large group of amateurs leaning the wrong way when a technical event – such as breaking a key moving average for a few periods – is all too obvious.

PERIOD	SHORT	INTERMEDIATE	LONG	CONFIRMATION
WEEK	10 (50 DAY)	20 (100 DAY)	40 (200 DAY)	
DAY	10	20	50	200
30 MIN	7	17	33	65 (5 DMA)
10 MIN	20	50	100	195 (5 DMA)
5 MIN	40	100	200	
2 MIN	20	50	100	
1 MIN	50	100		VWAP

Figure 10.4 This table shows the moving averages that best represent the short-, intermediate- and long-term trends for each timeframe. Sometimes a fourth average is added to gain a longer-term perspective and confirmation. These moving averages should not be viewed as literal levels for taking action, but as areas where price should be studied more closely.

Regardless of which timeframe is being studied, the cyclical structure of a market will create a rainbow look to it from the moving averages (see Figure 10.1). When price is viewed with these moving averages, you will notice certain relationships exhibited between price and the various moving averages. It is the interrelation of price and moving averages that allows you to clearly and objectively categorize the stage in which a stock "resides." The recognition and measurement of the presence of multiple trends on any given timeframe allows you to gain greater trend clarity, and the confidence from that analysis minimizes the chance of emotions entering your decision-making process.

I generally view three different moving averages on each timeframe, but sometimes add a fourth as a final confirmation of the longer-term trend. In order to keep my analysis of the trends consistent across various timeframes,

I color code the short-term moving averages with red, intermediate-term with blue and long-term trend with green. (Figure 10.5)

The shorter-term moving averages will always follow price action most closely as it takes less data to calculate. In other words, it is more sensitive to price movement. The short-term MA is considered to be "fast" because it responds most quickly to price change. The intermediate-term moving average will follow price next, and the longer-term moving average is considered to be the slowest because it pulls the most data into its calculation.

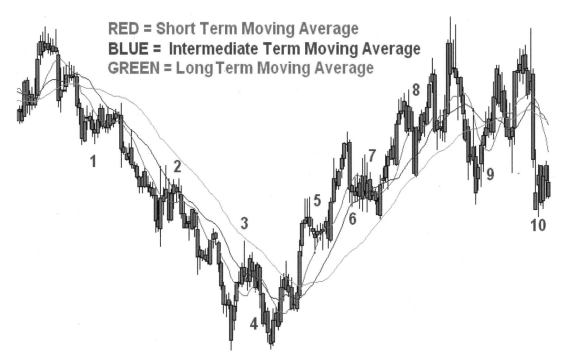

Figure 10.5 All reference to price and time has been removed from the chart above because it is meant to represent the relationship between price and the moving averages. The relationships described below are found on all timeframes with the moving averages in Figure 10.4. Please note that not all charts will look as symmetrical as this one. The trick, of course, is to find the ones where we have clear messages and avoid the stocks where the trend is not as clear. RealTick by Townsend Analytics.

Let's walk through the price/ moving average relationship which is present in nearly all markets and all timeframes.

1- After making a lower high and a lower low, the stock consolidates under the declining moving averages. Notice that the red short-term (ST) moving average (MA) is below the intermediate-term (INT) blue MA, which is below the longer-term (LT) green MA and that all of the MAs are declining. The stock is now in a confirmed Stage 4 decline.

2- As the stock continues lower, rallies are met with selling near the ST and INT MAs.

3- The further along the stock is in its decline, the stronger bounces become as short sellers scramble to lock in gains and new money is attracted to "bargain prices." The stock finds renewed selling near the LT *declining* MA.

4- The ST MA crosses above the INT MA, indicating a conflict between the ST trend and the longer trends. This indecision often comes as the stock searches for support; it shows disagreement among various timeframe participants relative to perception of value. *As long as the LT MA continues to trend lower, all rallies should be viewed with an eye of suspicion.* At this point the stock has entered Stage 1 accumulation, and trend traders should avoid the trendless action.

5- The stock establishes a higher high which is preceded by a higher low. The strength of this move carries the ST MA above the INT MA and the INT MA above the LT MA. The *direction* of all MAs is higher, and the stock is in a confirmed Stage 2 uptrend. Stocks at this point in the cycle should be studied on shorter-term timeframes for low-risk entry points as there is little evidence of sellers. When the ST>INT>LT MAs, a healthy uptrend is exhibited.

6- After initially finding support near the rising ST and INT MA, the pullbacks become deeper, and buyers are often found at longer term MAs.

7- The ST MA crosses below the INT MA, indicating a conflict between the three trends. This first sign of indecision should be treated cautiously with the *benefit of the doubt going to the buyers as long as the LT MA continues to advance.*

8- The stock recovers and trades to a new high, confirming that buyers never lost control of the LT trend.

9- The stock experiences a deeper pullback from all-time highs. As the volatility increases, the MAs send numerous conflicting messages as the frequency of crossovers increases, which when viewed together indicate indecision and a good stock of which to be wary.

10- The stock establishes a lower low that drags the declining ST MA down below the declining INT MA, which in turn crosses below the declining LT MA. The stock has completed a full cycle and is now in a confirmed Stage 4 decline.

By now you are probably looking at the referenced charts to determine which moving averages are best used on various timeframes. Please be reminded that moving averages are merely a reference point to which you should compare price, but should not be used as a system. There are no magic moving averages which work all the time. Nonetheless, there are ones that accurately and consistently represent the short-, intermediate- and long-term trends on various timeframes. Much of the value of moving averages comes from the fact that these MAs are the ones which are most commonly used, a fact that makes them most valuable for trying to anticipate the likely actions of the collective group of participants. The common recognition of any technical area or event brings about a self-fulfilling event as price approaches that area.

CHAPTER 11
TIME

Time is one of the few variables over which we have any control in our pursuit of market profits. The time we allow our market activities to work for (or against) us is completely subjective.

The goal of successful market timing is to avoid inactive sideways trading periods and be involved in stocks only when there is strong directional movement. When harnessed properly, you can use time to create incredible leverage for maximum percentage gains whether you are a short-term trader, a long-term investor or somewhere in between. In addition, using multiple timeframe analysis brings you closer to attaining the difficult-to-achieve goal of constant growth without drawdown.

The measurement of time, in life and in the stock market, is not one-dimensional. Man has identified numerous measurements of time from fractions of a second, to minutes, hours, days, weeks, months, years, decades, etc. Without any other reference, a simple statement such as "call me at three o'clock" has little value. Is that a.m. or p.m.? Which time zone, what day, this week? In the markets, measurement of time and trends is similarly ambiguous.

I often hear people say they are bullish or bearish, but without a reference to time those pronouncements have little value. Just as we measure time on many different levels, market activity must be studied on several timeframes to achieve the most objective analysis of trends. *The highest-probability trades are revealed when we do our analysis on multiple timeframes.*

The primary trend, of course, is the trend of the longest-term timeframe studied relative to the trade setup you are contemplating. The biggest money is made in the market when we follow the trend of the longer timeframes. As stated in the trend section, the fresher the primary trend is, the less likely it is to reverse, thus paving the way for larger profit opportunities with the least amount of risk. One of the keys to success is built on determining what represents the longer-term timeframe for *your* anticipated holding period.

If you are a longer-term planner, emotionally prepared for periods of underperformance in exchange for a lower level of attention to your investments, short-term trading probably has no appeal to you; it will take too much time and effort.   But if you cannot tolerate volatility of account balances and feel stupid for being in a stock as it experiences a normal correction of the prevailing trend, short-term trading allows for better control of performance consistency.

Some participants are attracted to the markets to fulfill a need for constant activity and relief of boredom, and that can be a dangerous motivation for trading. The only reason to trade is to make money. Between commission costs, which can add up quickly, and costly emotional decisions, the unprepared short-term trader has little chance of survival. To succeed in the market you need to thoroughly understand yourself and your motivations, and that means being introspective enough to study your reaction time and responses to constantly changing market information. An honest evaluation of your personal emotional "infrastructure" should help determine which timeframe best suits your emotional capacity.

Trend Alignment
The use of multiple timeframes to analyze a stock for low-risk, high-potential reward trend trades is a concept called "trend alignment." Because short-term and longer-term traders and investors hold different opinions of value and how quickly value may change, trends are measured on timeframes of varying length.

You are probably familiar with the market cliché "the trend is your friend," and for good reason.   For investors, longer-term wealth is created by participation in trends that can last for years. Achievement of consistent short-term trading profits is best accomplished by entering a stock in a longer-term trend just as the short-term trend confirms the longer term trend.

In theory, trend trading is simple -- buy low and sell high for longs and sell high and buy back lower for short positions. In reality, however, many traders find trend trading frustrating because they are not focused on the right trend, or they enter a position after a short-term move has already occurred.

A little over 100 years ago, Charles H. Dow wrote a series of editorials in the *Wall Street Journal* in which he laid out his views on how the stock market works. Collectively these writings are referred to as "The Dow Theory."   The work of Dow still holds water today, making it a key underpinning of technical analysis. One of the foundations of the Dow Theory is the identification of three types of price trends: the primary trend, the secondary trend and minor trends.

The **primary trend movements** are compared to "oceanic tides;" this constitutes the main trend of the market with a duration that can last a few months to several years. Primary trends cannot be manipulated as the forces of supply and demand are too large for any one participant to successfully influence the collective reasoning of the crowd.

Secondary movements, referred to as "waves," are reactionary moves within longer term trends, they typically last from two weeks to three months. Secondary movements are often created by a large participant/s (mutual funds, hedge funds, etc.) exiting a significant part of their positions. Once that supply (in an uptrend) is absorbed by the market, the buyers regain control, and the stock continues higher in the primary trend.

The third part of the Dow Theory surrounds **short-term (minor) trends**, viewed as insignificant ripples that last less than two weeks. Dow assigned little significance to these short-term trends because they represent fluctuations in the secondary trend. According to Dow, the short-term ripples in the market can be difficult to predict because they are often emotionally driven events. Today we know that skilled day traders can thrive on this type of emotional short-term movement.

Because there are at least three trends in a market, one of the most important elements to successful mastery of trend trading is to determine the right trend on which to focus. Timeframe choice is largely determined by individual factors including: your available time (to commit to the markets), your capital base, market experience and personal risk tolerance. As important is your patience level.

Investors are naturally attracted to the primary movement, while the secondary moves are more of a focus for intermediate-term participants (swing traders). Minor trends will be the obvious choice of day traders. As intuitive as that concept seems, it becomes more complicated because technical trading is about timing, and *time cannot be viewed one-dimensionally if you want the odds to stack up in your favor.*

Whether you fit behind door #1 (longer-term investor), door #2 (swing trader) or door #3 (day trader), a minimum of three timeframes should be referenced before a trade is made. I always begin my analysis by studying the longer-term trend because this allows me to understand the primary flow of capital and the path of least resistance. These longer, more powerful trends are the ones that you want to avoid fighting as mistakes will be magnified with larger losses. Thus, *the long-term timeframe is used for idea generation, not for timing purposes*.

For an investor, the timeframe to begin with is a weekly chart that encompasses at least two years of data. Swing traders can begin their trade candidate search on a daily timeframe, while the long term-trends from a day trader's perspective can be found on 30- minute timeframes.

	USE FOR	INVESTOR	SWINGTRADER	DAYTRADER
Primary Trend	Idea Generation	Week	Day	30 Minute
Secondary Trend	Establish Risk/Reward	Day	30 Minute	10/5 Minute
Minor Trend	Fine Tune Timing	30 Minute	10/5 Minute	2/1 Minute

Figure 11.1 The investor, swing trader and day trader will look at different timeframes for their analysis of primary, secondary and minor trends. These timeframes are meant as starting points. It is often necessary to look "further to the left" to see older data that may be relevant to the primary trend.

Once the stock has been identified as a viable trade candidate, the next step for a trade setup is to determine if there is sufficient potential for reward relative to the perceived risk to justify placing a trade. That's where the intermediate timeframe comes in; it helps you plan your trade by allowing you to better view the relevant levels of support and resistance in the market. The location of support and resistance levels in relation to current price lets you determine where stops should be placed (risk) and the potential level the stock may travel to (reward) if the market agrees with our analysis. The evaluation on an intermediate-term timeframe allows for easier recognition of levels of support and resistance that might not have been visible on the longer-term timeframe.

The intermediate-term trends are best recognized on a daily timeframe for investors, a 30-minute timeframe for swing traders and the 10/5-minute timeframes for day traders.

Once you have determined that there is a decent trade setup present, the short-term timeframe is your next source of consultation as that is where you will *make final timing decisions* to enter a trade. Studying the trends on the short-term timeframe allows you to become more precise in your entries, which ultimately leads to lower risk. The minor trends for investors are best recognized on the 30-minute timeframes, while swing traders will analyze the 10/5-minute timeframes, and day traders will focus on the developing trends on a 2/1-minute chart.

Note that the timeframes Charles Dow referred to were meant for investors. As technology and pricing has changed and opened more opportunities for shorter-term trading, today's swing trader would consider the daily timeframe to be the long-term (primary) trend and generally would want to trade in the direction of that trend. When I view the daily timeframe for a potential swing trade candidate, I like to analyze at least 150 days of data to get a good feel for the longer-term dominant trend.

The intermediate-term timeframes for a swing trader are best recognized on charts that use 30-minute data. For the intermediate-term timeframe, I typically analyze 20 to 30 days of trading activity. The short-term trend for a swing trader can be found on a 5- or 10- minute timeframe. I typically view five days for the 5-minute data and ten days for the 10-minute data. See Figure 11.1 for which timeframes are most appropriate for day traders and investors.

Even day traders will be able to benefit from studying a minimum of three timeframes. For a day trader, the trend spanning 20 to 30 days on a 30-minute chart typically is sufficient to understand the longer-term forces at work in the stock. For the intermediate-term determination of key levels of potential support and resistance relevant to their anticipated time to hold the stock, the day trader will benefit most from studying the 5-10 minute timeframes for the previous five to ten days. To gain more precise entries and exits, the day trader will study the one- and two-minute timeframes for the preceding day or two.

Regardless of how you categorize yourself -- investor, swing trader or day trader -- stay focused on the timeframes relevant to your style. If you are an investor or even a swing trader, studying one- and two-minute timeframes can seduce you into taking more trades than necessary for your style; this can result in overtrading with higher commission costs and missed opportunities.

For a day trader, analyzing the longer-term timeframes (such as weekly charts) will add little value – and may even do harm by allowing complacency to develop as you justify holding what was supposed to be a short-term trade based on longer-term trends. Always be aware of all of the forces in the market, but learn to focus *only* on the timeframes relevant to your objectives.

Here's an overview of the rules:

- Regardless of whether you are an investor, swing trader or day trader, a minimum of three timeframes should be studied before you commit capital to a trade.

- The greater the number of timeframes you study to confirm the trend, the greater the probability that your trade will succeed as you become aware of more potential outcomes.

- Decisions to buy or sell should be based on the shorter-term timeframes as they tend to lead the longer-term trends. The long-term trend is nothing more than the sum of the shorter-term trends, so the short-term trends lead the longer-term trends.

- Using a minimum of three different timeframes for analysis aids three ways: identify the primary trend (long term), establish a risk/reward ratio using recent support and resistance levels (intermediate term), hone in on more accurate entries (short term).

The concept of utilizing multiple timeframes for trading is one that every market participant should consider because it allows for a greater level of objective analysis based on what the market is *actually doing* rather than relying on our opinions as related to trading decisions. In the end, multiple timeframes allow us to become better at holding our winners and cutting our losers, a goal common to all market participants.

And Finally…
There is a tendency for traders to feel as if they have to be continually engaged in a position, but when there are mixed trend signals across various

timeframes, it is best to revert to a more cautious mode until trends begin to align and show lower-risk entries.

Also remember that while it is true that individual stock trends are largely influenced by the trends of the general market and the sector of which they are a part, there are always going to be stocks that trade without those influences. There are times in both bull and bear markets where some individual stocks will become immune to overall market strength and weakness, respectively. In nasty bear markets there are winners, and in strong bull markets there will be losers. Focus on the trends of the stock you are trading, not on a relationship which is "supposed to be present." If you focus on the theoretical relationships that many academics debate, you will often find yourself asking how the market can be so wrong.

The point is to be aware of the anomalies present within and across different asset classes, but trade what you see, not what you think should happen. If you have a difficult time believing what you see in an individual stock, simply stand aside. Only price pays, and fighting a trend based on seemingly "logical" reasoning has led many a contrarian to go out of business.

CHAPTER 12
HOW & WHEN TO BUY

In order to attain larger winners than losers, the easiest way to stack the odds in your favor is to trade with the primary trend, whether up or down. These are the lowest-risk, highest-profit-potential setups. The most basic definition of an uptrend – with higher highs and higher lows – means that the sum of the rallies will always be greater than the sum of the declines. That's the kind of math we want to follow.

Most investors are enamored with trends to the upside, and we'll discuss the basics behind these moves in this chapter. But as we watch bear markets typically slide faster than bull markets climb, descending markets are not to be ignored. That's why the following chapter focuses on the short side. The nature of each is incredibly important to the savvy investor and trader.

Whether long or short, the adherence to simple trend alignments rules with the primary trend should be our guide. Attempts to pick tops and bottoms are much higher-risk trades that require a high risk tolerance and extreme emotional control.

For a trend trader, the only stocks which should be of *any interest* are those in an established Stage 2 Uptrend or a Stage 4 Decline. Let's then combine the analysis of price, volume and moving averages on multiple timeframes to identify the ideal long and short trading candidates for a swing traders timeframe. The same concepts we use for swing trades can be used by investors and day traders by using the indicated timeframes in the table below. We will start with long-side trades and then examine examples of short sales in Chapter 13.

As laid out regarding time and timeframes in Chapter 11, the classification of trend varies among various participants. Below (Figure 12.1) is another look at the table of some of the most relevant timeframes for investors, swing traders and day traders. Again, the concepts of trend alignment do not apply to just short-term trading. Correct identification of the primary trend for idea generation, the intermediate-term trends for assessing risk/reward and the short-term trends for trade entries is a concept that can help all market participants minimize risk and maximize gains. *While no method of trading exists that assures only winning trades, analysis of multiple timeframes allows us to participate in the dominant market trends while controlling risks on the shorter timeframes.*

	USE FOR	INVESTOR	SWINGTRADER	DAYTRADER
Primary Trend	Idea Generation	Week	Day	30 Minute
Secondary Trend	Establish Risk/Reward	Day	30 Minute	10/5 Minute
Minor Trend	Fine Tune Timing	30 Minute	10/5 Minute	2/1 Minute

Figure 12.1 Another look at timeframes.

It would be irresponsible of me not to point out the potential for danger in analyzing even shorter timeframes. It is easy to be seduced by the seemingly easy and fast moves on these shorter timeframe cousins. However, just as you must learn to crawl before you walk and walk before you run, you must first master trading on the longer-term timeframes before applying the techniques to shorter timeframes.

The greatest value to shorter-term analysis is the reduction of risk by capturing more accurate entries and managing stops. The biggest setbacks to successful short-term trading are the extreme concentration and quick thinking necessary to avoid making emotional decisions. Maintaining discipline and emotional detachment is more important than trying to catch every move you see, and no one catches them all.

Daily Timeframe: Identify the Stock
The first consideration for a stock to trade to the long side is that it must be in a Stage two uptrend on the daily timeframe.

For a swing trade candidate, we begin our search on the daily timeframes for a pattern of higher highs and higher lows. The best candidates are those stocks that are trading above the rising 10-, 20- and 50-day moving averages, with the moving averages stacked above each other 10>20>50. Consider it a bonus if the stock is above all of the rising key (10, 20, 40) moving averages on the weekly timeframe. However, note that for a short-term trader, by the time the trends of the weekly timeframe become relevant, it is likely the trade may have been exited.

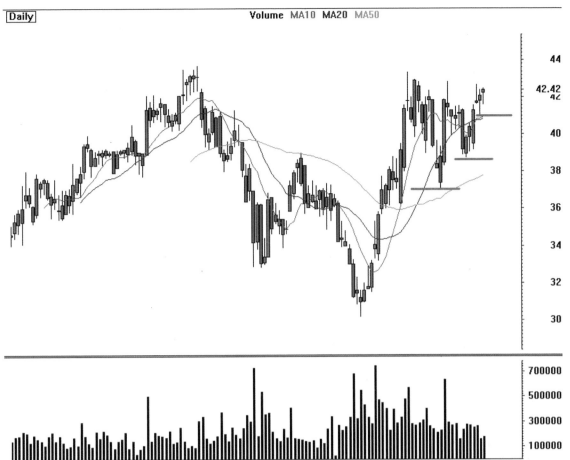

Figure 12.2 The stock on this daily timeframe is in a clear uptrend with rising 10-, 20- and 50-day moving averages. The recent support at the 10- and 20-day moving averages forms the higher low where an initial protective stop would be placed. Because the stock is trading near new highs, our minimum upside target would be 44.50 (a conservative target which assumes a slight movement into new high territory). The 30-minute and 10- minute charts of the same stock are shown in Figure 12.3 and 12.4, respectively. RealTick by Townsend Analytics

30-Minute Timeframe: Assess the Risk/Reward

Once a stock has been identified as a potential long trade candidate, the next step is to drill our analysis down to an intermediate-term timeframe such as a 30-minute chart showing 15 to 20 days of data (Figure 12.3). *The primary objective on the intermediate term timeframe is to identify potential support and resistance levels to determine risk/reward ratio.* Any stop strategy is better than a market approach that does not deal with the possibility of loss, but it is a mistake to base long stops on anything other than actual levels of prior support. When you enter a stock where you anticipate upside activity, you want to buy at the onset of short-term strength and hold as long as the uptrend remains intact.

As a new trend begins and you enter a long position, your first objective is capital preservation, and the initial protective stop assures that any loss will be acceptable based on the perceived risk/reward ratio. The most sensible stop for a new long position is one that is simply based on the definition of a long trend -- "higher highs and higher lows." If the stock violates the important level of support prior to entry on the 30-minute timeframe, there is no longer any reason to be holding long as the definition of trend is no longer valid. *Once the definition of trend is invalidated and you continue to hold the stock, you are no longer a trend trader.*

Figure 12.3 The 30-minute timeframe allows us to see that the stock would break the resistance near 42.50. With the most recent higher low being near 41.80, our risk would be 70 cents versus our anticipated reward of 2.00. RealTick by Townsend Analytics.

By the way, stops are of no value if you do not take action. It is easy to manufacture reasons to justify a continued hold of the stock, but that is an amateurish mindset. Forget your opinion of the company. Don't pay attention to the volume or any other seemingly logical reasons to continue to hold. These excuses are your way of not admitting defeat. When the stock makes a lower low, plain and simple it signals that buyers did not have the power to overcome selling pressure, and the stock will need to correct further, either price-wise or through time.

The 30-minute timeframe not only allows us to clearly identify important support levels on which to base our stops, but it gives us a clearer picture of potential sources of supply where the stock may find resistance that portends a halt to the upward momentum. A large-volume consolidation that, for example, lasted for four hours before the stock broke down will not show as a potential resistance level if you are looking solely at a daily timeframe; it is the analysis of intraday timeframes that allows us to identify these key levels. Don't look at four hours literally here. The point is this: *a prior significant level of trading that may not be visible on the longer timeframe may become a point where future supply is released to the market and upward momentum is interrupted.* Because these levels may halt a short-term uptrend, they can be the basis of the upside target and justify taking a trade relative to the perceived risk.

The 10-Minute/5-Minute Stalk the Trade
Once an acceptable risk/reward ratio has been determined on the intermediate-term timeframe, the next step is to *identify short-term trends to establish a more precise buying point and then to manage the open trade.* When we observe the presence of the four stages on the 10-minute timeframe, our actions to buy and sell will be dictated by those stages.

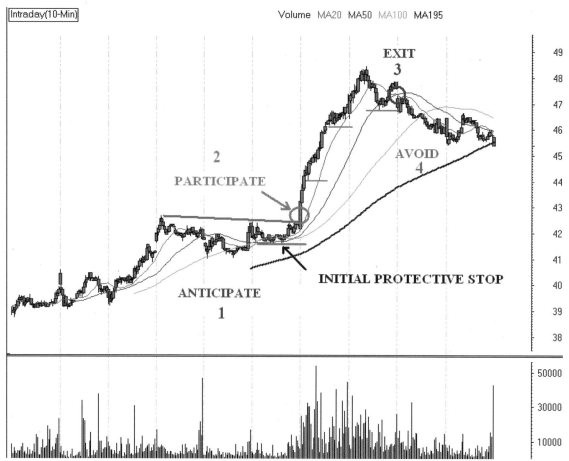

Figure 12.4 The 10-minute timeframe identifies the break past short-term resistance at the circled level, which attracted a surge in buying. When a stock moves this rapidly I often place a trailing stop on a small portion of the trade, which allows the position to remain open during the rapid momentum. When a stock moves this rapidly, it is difficult to identify solid levels to raise your stop, so each small pullback must be monitored very closely. As the stock recovers from the short-term corrections, the low of the correction serves as the location of the new stop. The process of raising stops is continued until the stock trades to a lower low on this timeframe or until the moving averages cross and show indecision. RealTick by Townsend Analytics.

With the primary trend being a Stage 2 uptrend, and the risk/reward having been established on a 30-minute timeframe, the 10-minute timeframe provides our action points as explained below.

Stage 1- Anticipate. When the daily trend of the stock is Stage 2, *the observation of Stage 1 accumulation on the 10-minute timeframe is the time to be on high alert for buyers to regain control of the short-term trend.* These stocks are the ones with the greatest likelihood of near-term upside movement; but it is not yet time to buy. The short-term Stage 1 represents indecision, and although the primary risk in these stocks is time, there is no guarantee that the stock will continue higher; at this point premature entries will expose you to unnecessary risk, but stay alert. The short-term area of indecision should be watched closely, and you should be actively "stalking the stock."

By stalking the stock before it makes a move, you will be in a position to observe unfolding market activity closely and determine the ideal entry point as the stock transitions from a period of short-term indecision to the very beginning of a new potential move higher. No action should be taken to get long until the stock begins to move higher on the shorter timeframes. The market phrase, "when in doubt, stay out" should be paramount here. Just as moving average crossovers represent indecision on one particular timeframe, the lack of aligned trends shows us a lack of consensus among participants of varying timeframes. This lack of consensus creates conflicting trends on various timeframes that diminishes the odds of a sustainable tradable move. In other words, if timeframes aren't aligned, being in cash gives us the ability to maintain an objective look at the stock. It is best to wait for confirmation from price and time before speculating on a move in the direction of the primary trend.

While the stock is in Stage 1, look closely at increasing volume, higher lows, and more frequent tests of short-term resistance signal buyers potentially becoming more aggressive.

Short-term Stage 1 is the time to set alerts to avoid missing out on the move if you are watching other open positions. If I think the stock will break resistance at a literal number such as 25.30, I will set my alert for 25.26 or some other number just below the key level. Being alerted to the stock as it gets close to a breakout assures that I will have my eyes on the trading activity just before a break into an uptrend. If I wait for the breakout to occur before I begin to watch the stock closely and do not have orders loaded to buy, I may end up being late and have to chase the stock higher.

As you wait for Stage 1 to complete, watch the L2 screen for speed and size of trades. You should observe where the supply is offered, how much size is offered, and if the offers look real (or conversely, if they are hiding bigger size that will prevent the stock from rallying). It is only during those last moments – studying the actions in the Level 2 screen -- that I decide whether or not to purchase the stock.

Stage 2 – Participate. *Once the stock has broken past the short-term level of resistance and has established a higher high, it is time to buy!* This first higher high confirms buyer dominance, and buying here gets us involved in the unfolding strength right at the beginning of the short-term uptrend. It is the point at which new upward momentum is revealed and where the short-term trend is established. As has been shown historically, *a trend once established is more likely to continue than to reverse.* This is particularly true when the trends from multiple timeframes become aligned with an established uptrend on the longer-term timeframe now confirmed by the shorter-term activity.

Stalking the stock in the short-term accumulation will put you in a position to observe and anticipate the moment when buyers reestablish their control, and you likely will be among the first participants to set foot in the new move. Note that it is a common mistake to wait for volume to confirm price activity of the higher high on the short-term timeframe; large-volume levels will not yet be present as trading activity typically increases *after* prices have experienced short term price movement.

Once the stock has been purchased, the next step is to closely observe the trading activity for confirmation of trend sustenance. I have heard people say that "winners take care of themselves," and I do not agree with it. To mitigate losses and maximize profitability of each trade, the stock needs to be managed *aggressively*. To maximize gains, you want to allow the stock to experience normal corrections (which do not violate the prior higher low) on the 10-minute timeframe before deciding to exit.

After an initial short-term burst of buying activity, I typically exit a small portion of my position. I may decide to exit one-fourth to one-third of my position on the first thrust higher because it allows me to be in a position of strength after I have already banked a small amount of profits. If the unfolding short-term uptrend rally fails and then reverses., the small realized profits assure I will not lose money on the trade if I move my stop to breakeven on the balance. I am a big believer in reducing risk at every opportunity, and selling a portion of my shares early on accomplishes that.

On the other hand, if the stock continues higher and my position is not stopped out, my job is to be patient enough to allow the stock to continue higher and to raise my stops as the market dictates. As long as the stock continues to establish a pattern of higher highs and higher lows on the 10-minute timeframe, there is no reason to exit. The pattern of finding successively higher levels of support on pullbacks near the short-, intermediate- and longer-term moving averages should also provide clues as to the strength of the trend. If the pullbacks become deeper than you would expect, your level of caution should increase, and your finger should be closer to the exit button.

As price targets are met, I typically exit another portion of my position. If there is truly resistance to be found at my target, selling a portion of the stock allows me to book profits while there is still sufficient liquidity to exit. In addition, my selling doesn't push the stock lower.

Stage 3 - Exit. As we know, an uptrend will correct in one of two ways. The first is price, if the stock violates the previous higher low on the 10-minute timeframe, the short-term trend becomes invalidated. I view that as my cue to exit any remaining long shares.

The other way stocks correct is through time. *A time correction often will continue in the direction of the primary trend*, but when the 10-minute timeframe shows the first signs of indecision (short-term moving average crossing below intermediate-term moving average), I exit any remaining shares of the stock. A short-term Stage 3 correction does not always lead to lower prices; however, it does signal a period where the rate of change has lost momentum, and it is unlikely for the stock to continue higher in the short term.

Short-term trend trading is about capturing trading profits while the stock is moving and avoiding the periods of indecision. When the momentum wanes, I take that as a signal to exit any remaining shares. When I exit the stock, it does not mean I have lost all interest in it. These levels of consolidation may last a day or two and then take off back to the upside. I make it a point to keep an eye on the stock by moving it to a watch list that I'll check two to three times per day. The short-term distribution indicates a minimum of further time consolidation, but it often leads to a deeper price correction.

Stage 4 - Avoid. When the short-term trend of the stock shows lower highs and lower lows, consider it a bear market for the short-term trader, and avoid the stock. It is possible to make money by selling short those stocks experiencing a short-term price decline in an overall uptrend, but the risks are much higher than shorting a stock where the primary trend is lower. Again, the simple math reminds us that the dominant uptrend will offer less opportunity to profit from the sum of the declines than the sum of the short-term rallies.

It is also risky to short these stocks because your position is more likely to be negatively impacted by news releases. Remember that "news and surprises tend to follow the primary trend," and the longer-term uptrend favors the likelihood of a fundamentally solid company where good news is often released.

When the longer-term trend is higher and the short-term trend is lower, the trends of the varying timeframes are showing directional conflict, and the stock should not be entered. Instead of attempting to "scale in" or "average down," a long candidate should be allowed to experience the full short-term Stage 4 decline on the 10-minute timeframe before it is even considered a long candidate. *We never know if a stock will find support and then bounce; buying into a short-term decline puts you in an immediate and unnecessary losing position.*

Below is another example of a trade setup on the long side using three timeframes.

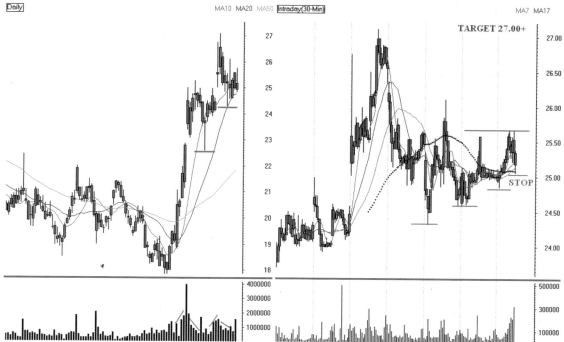

Figure 12.5 The daily and 30- minute timeframe are viewed side by side to display the consolidation of the dominant Stage 2 uptrend in greater detail. The initial risk/ reward ratio is determined by anticipating a move past short-term resistance near 25.60 with a stop below the recent higher low near 25.00. The potential reward is based on the likelihood of the daily uptrend to exceed the prior high at 27.00. RealTick by Townsend Analytics.

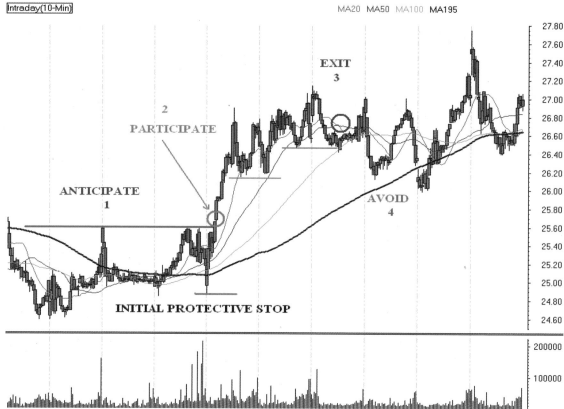

Figure 12.6 The 10-minute timeframe shows us the point where the stock establishes a short-term higher high, giving a reason to purchase the stock as the short-term trend is now aligned with the daily trend. The stock travels up just above 27.00 before establishing a lower low, which is followed soon after by a moving average crossover. While the stock eventually recovered and continued higher, the exit at the lower low allowed for an exit as momentum subsided, thereby avoiding three days of choppy action before buyers were able to regain control of the trend. RealTick by Townsend Analytics.

CHAPTER 13
HOW & WHEN TO SELL SHORT

If you are serious about making consistent profits in the markets, you want to be able to profit in any market environment, not just when stocks are rising. I am often surprised by how many people approach me and tell me they are interested in a trading career but have no experience selling short. More shocking is that they have absolutely no interest in selling short.

This potentially cuts these long-only participants' opportunities in half. Though I have done no independent verification of studies, it is said that bear markets occur every 39 months on average and that they typically last for about 18 months. That is a lot of time where the odds are stacked against long trades and where selling short makes sense to generate market profits for the purpose of current income.

Bear markets bring about a return to realistic expectations after an "easy" bull market sends participants' confidence levels soaring. It is said that bull markets will bail you out of careless trades, while bear markets will punish any slip of discipline. Bull market traders are reminded of the fact that stocks are risky in a bearish environment, while disciplined and flexible traders continue to rack up profits as prices decline.

Selling short is a strategy which to attempts to capture profits from a declining stock. By selling first, the trader expects to profit by repurchasing the shares at a lower level and profiting from the difference. Short sales are generally considered to be riskier than buying stock long because of the possibility of unlimited losses. If you buy a stock at $20/share, the most you can lose is $20/share, while if you sell short you can lose much more if the stock advances. There is nothing to prevent the stock from trading up to $30, $50 or $100/share, or higher!

Clearly, cutting losses must be taken very seriously when selling short. While it is true that in theory you can lose more money than you invest in a short sale and that your risk exposure is unlimited in a short position, proper position sizing and risk management greatly mitigate the potential for a catastrophic outcome when selling short.

Upticks and Exchange-Traded Funds

Establishing a short position has become easier due to rule changes and with the introduction of innovative Exchange Traded Funds (ETFs). On July 6, 2007, the short sale rules were changed, making it easier to short stocks with the elimination of the "uptick rule." The uptick rule was part of the Securities Exchange Act of 1934, which permitted short selling only following a trade where the price was higher than the previously traded price.

In 2006, inverse and double-inverse ETFs were introduced to the trading community. Inverse ETF products allow market participants to go long a securities exchange-traded product and gain exposure to the downside. The double-inverse ETFs give participants two times the short exposure, meaning that if the primary ETF drops one percent, the double-inverse ETF *gains* two percent. Leverage is also offered to long traders with double percentage exposure offered in various indices.

These products are available for most major market indices as well as a growing number of sector funds. They have become very popular as many participants find it more comforting to bet against the market by going long. Their popularity also has been boosted by leverage as they are able to be traded with "qualified money" such as IRA accounts. Traditional short sales and leveraged positions are restricted from being traded with retirement funds due to rules against using margin in retirement accounts. A short sale must be initiated in a margin account, and because margin trades are restricted in retirement accounts, the ability to sell short was also restricted.

Shorting Takes the Right Mindset

To the average market participant, bear markets are brutal periods that drain their equity and emotions. Some investors have learned to recognize downtrends and successfully position themselves in cash, thereby avoiding the carnage that so many long-only participants experience. Traders who earn their living from the markets obviously cannot wait for their positions to come back or even afford the luxury of time sitting idle on the sidelines with waiting cash. This is why selling short is a skill that every serious trader learns to utilize during Stage 4 market declines.

The truth is, short selling is a legitimate strategy for making money in the markets, and if you trade the market actively, not having short exposure can be like fighting with one hand tied behind your back. Yet many intertwining emotions and age-old perceptions remain. Many participants find trading the short side of the market to be nerve wracking. For the traditional buy-low-sell-high mindset, it can feel unnatural to sell something that you do not own. In addition, short sellers have been criticized as being un-American or un-patriotic. From an emotional standpoint, some participants feel bad about profiting from the shortcomings of a company or making money when long participants are losing.

Don't feel bad about how you make a living. Active trading is about making consistent profits, and you must be capable of exploiting any edge you can find, including betting against a stock where there are obvious signs of mass liquidation.

The best time to sell short is during a bear market, but there are always stocks in a Stage 4 decline that can be sold short regardless of the overall market environment.

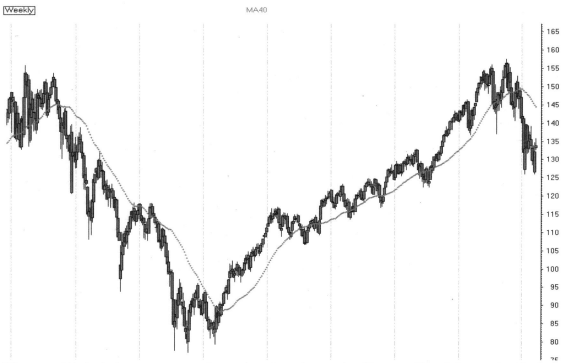

Figure 13.1 A longer-term bear market is typically confined by a declining 40-week (200-day) moving average. RealTick by Townsend Analytics.

But what exactly is a bear market? Many people consider a ten percent or greater broad market decline to be an official bear market, but I consider that to be too loose of a definition. Without trying to precisely define a bear market, the most obvious sign of market bearishness is when the majority of stocks are in established downtrends or when the overall market indices are below key moving averages. The best way to define a bear market is an environment in which markets where the 200-day MA is declining. (Figure 13.1)

The fact is, stocks tend to drop much quicker than they advance and it has a great deal to do with emotion. *Bear markets are characterized by a stronger emotional response than bull markets because people are complacent when they are winning and become frightened when they are losing.* Fear is a much stronger motivator than complacency, and emotional liquidation from frustrated long holders can lead to quick declines.

Fear of the longs often shows its first signs as the stock experiences an unusually large drop on huge volume -- loosely defined as at least five times larger than the average trading volume of the last 20 days. When stocks are "thrown away" all at once on large volume, it signals a shift in the perception of the participants. Often the catalyst for such a move is a fundamental event. These stocks become potential shorting candidates and they are worth keeping an eye on over the next several months while stubborn longs continue to sell their positions out of frustration.

Choosing Shorts
As a general rule, you should be much choosier for short trading candidates than a corresponding long. When it comes to trading the short side, your timing needs to be more accurate, and you definitely will not get away with sloppy trading as much as you would in a bull market. Marginal setups that may have worked in a bull market are an anathema to bear markets, in which you need to be much more careful and disciplined.

In a bear environment, try to concentrate only on the highest-probability setups, and keep overall trading activity low relative to your trading volume in a bull market. *You need to have the patience to let the market present you with the lowest-risk opportunities.* Not surprisingly, this occurs when the trends are aligned on multiple timeframes.

Smaller share size in bear markets is another general rule. Think survival first in a bear market as the "squeeze rallies" can do as much damage as holding on to a losing long trade during the decline. Liquidity can become thin in a squeeze environment, and large share size makes it very difficult to exit a position without creating a negative market impact cost. *Some of the sharpest rallies experienced by stocks occur during a downtrend*, and while these rallies usually fail to hold up in a down trending stock, there is no excuse to hold on to a position where you are experiencing excruciating losses. The short squeeze rallies are borne from a high level of emotion that starts with a little bargain buying and then lures more sidelined cash to the long side for fear of missing the bottom. This slowly building momentum tempts weak shorts (like me) to cover before profits erode and losses mount. As this buying pressure builds, the supply is also withdrawn from the market and other shorts begin to chase the stock higher. The now-greedy long players press their long hand by purchasing more shares, reveling in delight that the "evil" short sellers are getting a good dose of pain.

These rallies are not built on a solid foundation of "natural longs" looking to hold long term and typically fail in short order, which is why all but the most aggressive and disciplined traders should go anywhere near them. Trend trading is the safer way to consistent profitability, so do not allow yourself to be enticed by the rapid movement. Instead, the truly astute trend following short seller waits for this type of rally to fizzle out before reestablishing a short position.

Short Alignment
Trend alignment of short trading positions is the lowest-risk, highest-profit potential trade scenario. Whether we trade long or short, the basic cyclical structure of the market never changes. As you will undoubtedly notice in the next section, there are many similarities between trading long and short in the setup, initiation and maintenance of a trade.

The examples in this chapter will refer to the swing trader timeframes, if you plan on selling short with different timeframes, the table in Figure 12.1 should be used to establish the correct timeframes for your objectives.

Stage 4 – Daily Timeframe - Identify Trade Candidate
The first step in trading short is to find a stock in an established Stage 4 downtrend. When trading from the short side, we ideally want the overall market, the sector and the stock to be in a decline. Just as we look for alignment across different timeframes, higher-probability short sales are encountered in sectors where there is overall weakness. When there is broad weakness in a sector, it greatly mitigates the risk that the decline in a stock is a one-time, short-lived problem specific to one company's stock.

For a swing trade candidate, we begin our search on the daily timeframes for a pattern of lower highs and lower lows. The best candidates are those stocks which are trading below the declining 10-, 20- and 50-day moving averages, with the moving averages stacked below each other 10<20<50. It is a better setup if the stock is also below the key moving averages on the longer term (weekly) timeframe, but do not exclude a stock from being a swing trade candidate because of the trends on the weekly timeframe. By the time the trends of the weekly timeframe become relevant, it is likely the trade will be exited. Consider it a bonus if the stock is below all of the declining key moving averages on the weekly timeframe. If that sounds familiar, it should, it is the mirror image of what we would look for in a long side trade setup.

Figure 13.2 The stock above is in a clear downtrend with declining 10-, 20- and 50-day moving averages. This stock becomes a good target for short sales. RealTick by Townsend Analytics.

30-Minute Timeframe

Once a stock has been identified as a potential short trade candidate, the next step is to drill down to an intermediate-term timeframe such as a 30-minute chart showing 15 to 20 days of data. The primary objective on the intermediate-term timeframe is to identify potential resistance and support levels to determine the risk/reward ratio based on stock action.

When you enter a short position, you want to sell short at the onset of short-term weakness and stay short as long as the downtrend remains intact. *As a new downtrend begins, your first objective is capital preservation, and the initial protective stop assures that any loss will be acceptable based on the perceived risk/reward ratio.* The most sensible stop for a short position is one based on the definition of a downtrend -- "lower highs and lower lows." If the stock violates the important level of resistance on the 30-minute timeframe, there is no longer any reason to remain short as the definition of trend is no longer valid. Once trend is invalidated and you continue to hold the stock, you are no longer a trend trader. When the stock makes a higher high, it signals that buyers have taken control of the short-term trend, which eliminates any edge you might have had in a short position.

The 30-minute timeframe not only allows us to clearly identify important resistance levels on which to base our stops, but it also gives us a clearer picture of potential sources of demand where the stock may find support as it renews its downward momentum. These levels become the basis of establishing a downside price objective.

When we establish a risk/reward scenario prior to entry, we should ask two questions: *Where has the stock come from and where does it have the potential to go?* The answer to where the stock has come from gives us the opportunity to make sure that we are not chasing prices lower in a stock that has already experienced a short-term decline. We want to enter the position after a period of low volatility where a potential source of supply is close by to halt the stock (the most recent lower high) if it rallies instead of declines.

The question of where the stock has the potential to go is based on the most significant level of support on the 30-minute timeframe and is meant to give us an objective downside price target. Naturally, we hope the stock will crash through all levels of potential support when we are short, but we need to keep our emotions out of the equation as much as possible and be alert to the areas where momentum may slow.

Figure 13.3 A closer look at the stock in the Stage 4 decline on the daily timeframe (Figure 13.2) confirms weakness. The 30-minute timeframe above shows a declining 65 period (5-day) moving average and recent resistance near 73.50. A stop just above 73.50 (1.80/risk per share) would nullify the downtrend, and a stop should be placed just above that level. Because the primary trend found on the daily timeframe is lower, we would expect the stock to continue to establish "lower lows" as a price target. In an attempt to be conservative with our downside objective, we will look for the stock to drop down towards the recent low near 67.00 (4.50 points away). Because we use the prior low as a target instead of a lower low, the risk/reward ratio of 1:2.5 would be acceptable to justify a short trade. RealTick by Townsend Analytics.

Stalking the Trade: 10-Minute/5-Minute

Once an acceptable risk/reward ratio has been determined on the intermediate-term timeframe, the next step is to identify short-term trends to establish a more precise selling point and then to manage the open trade. When we observe the presence of the four stages on the 10-minute timeframe, our actions to buy and sell will be guided by those stages. In a short sale candidate, we begin our most careful analysis and begin to stalk the stock for an entry point as it enters the Stage 3 distribution.

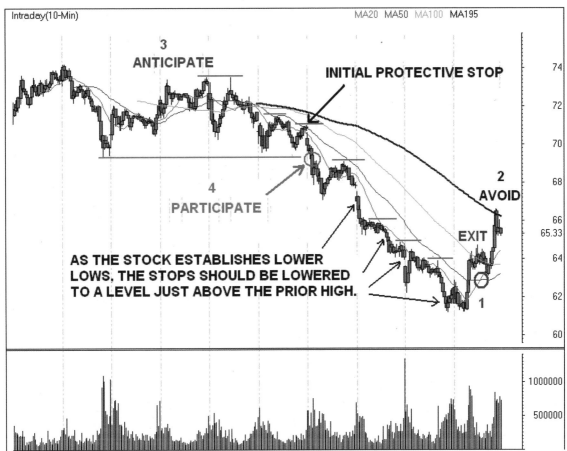

Figure 13.4 The same stock we analyzed on the daily and 30-minute timeframes is shown after the stock broke down on this 10-minute timeframe. The correct entry came as the stock created a lower low near 69.00. The most recent lower high at this point was found near 71.00, and the stop placement should have been just above that level. You can see how the stock quickly dropped another two dollars; that initial drop is an excellent time to cover a partial position to lock in a little profit and reduce overall risk. After the stock partially recovered from the initial drop, the sellers forced it to new lows again. As new lows are established, the stop on the remaining shares should be methodically lowered to a level just above the preceding high. You can see that the stock was stopped out near 64.00 (about 5 points lower and exceeding the initial conservative target). The higher high near 64.00 was also responsible for the circled moving average crossover, which would give us another reason to lock in gains. RealTick by Townsend Analytics.

For short sales, we always want to begin our analysis with the study of a Stage 4 decline stock on the daily timeframe. The next step is to establish a risk/reward ratio on the 30-minute timeframe. Finally we observe the action on the 10-minute timeframe with the appropriate actions for each short term stage described below.

Stage 3- Anticipate

When the daily trend of the stock is Stage 4, the observation of Stage 3 accumulation on the 10-minute timeframe signals it is time to be on high alert for sellers to regain control of the short-term trend. *When a stock in a primary (daily) downtrend is being distributed on a 10-minute timeframe, it is the most likely time to begin a new leg lower.* However, it is too early to enter because the stock does not yet show the downside momentum.

The short-term Stage 3 represents indecision, and the most likely form of risk is that of time. Nonetheless, there are times when these stocks do reverse higher, and an early entry can be costly. At this area of indecision, you should be actively "stalking the stock" by looking for signs that sellers may becoming more aggressive. *Be alert for signs of increased volume, lower highs and more frequent tests of short-term support.*

Stage 4 - Participate

Once the stock has broken below the short-term level of support from the distribution and has established a lower low, it is time to sell the stock. This first lower low establishes sellers' control, and entering the trade at this point gets us involved in the developing weakness *just as the move begins.* It is the point at which new downward momentum is revealed and where the short-term downtrend is established. As we know, a trend once established is more likely to continue than to reverse. This is particularly true when the trends from multiple timeframes become aligned; sellers control the long-, intermediate- and short-term trends.

I always use limit orders to enter a short position, but it doesn't always have to be at the current bid. Sometimes if it looks as though the stock is breaking down and bids are thin, I use a leading limit order that gives a little more room for the order to be filled. For example, if the current bid is 500 shares at 25.50, with another 300 shares bid at 25.48, 600 at 25.47 and 200 at 25.45, I may enter an order to sell short 2,000 shares with a limit of 25.45. This type of order would clear all of the liquidity (total of 1,600 shares) down to 25.45, with the remaining 400 shares becoming the inside (best) offer price. In that scenario, someone would be required to purchase the stock at that level for my order to be completely filled.

Using a leading limit order has a few advantages in this situation. First, I will be able to "steal" liquidity from other, slower-to-react traders. Second, my aggressive action at a key level may further influence other participants to pull their bids from the market or for other shorts to chase the stock lower.

Once a short position has been established, the next step is to observe the trading activity for confirmation of the trend being sustained. Referring again to the definition of a downtrend -- lower highs and lower lows – you want to allow the stock to experience *normal corrections* (which do not violate the prior lower highs) on the 10-minute timeframe before deciding to exit with a profit.

I treat short positions in the same as way as I treat long positions to realize profits. After a quick short-term sell off, I typically exit a small portion of my position on the first decline – as much as one-fourth to one-third of the total – because it allows me to be in a position of strength in the stock. If the unfolding short-term downtrend suddenly reverses and the stock turns higher, I hopefully have extracted enough of a profit to allow my stop to be moved to breakeven on the balance of the position. Further, it gives me the assurance that if my position gets stopped out, I will not lose any money. If, on the other hand, the balance of my position is not stopped out, my job is to be patient enough to allow the stock to continue to decline and to *lower my stops as the action of the stock dictates.*

Buy stops should be placed at sensible chart-based levels. Again using the definition of a downtrend, I set a stop just above the most recent level at which the market found resistance. As long as the stock continues to establish a pattern of lower highs and lower lows on the 10-minute timeframe, there is no logical reason to exit the entire short position. Be quick to take your losses if a buy stop is hit, and do not make the mistake of canceling your order and reassessing risk levels. If you do the proper analysis prior to entering a trade, you cannot allow your emotions to be influenced by new price action. Once the plan is in place, do not change it if price goes against you momentarily. The only time stops should be changed on short trades is when the market moves in your favor and you are reducing risk by lowering the stop or to assure that gains are being protected. A short squeeze can happen very rapidly, and the small loss from your initial stop is far more favorable than allowing a loser to spiral out of control. Remember that large losses are unacceptable!

As price targets are met, I typically exit yet another portion of my position. If there is truly support to be found at my target, buying back a portion of the stock allows me to book profits while there is still sufficient liquidity to exit without my buying pushing the stock higher.

It is a great feeling to profit when you are short a stock that reports bad news. As we know, news and surprises tend to follow the direction of the trend, and news also tends to be released towards the end of a short-term move. If you are lucky enough to be short a stock that gaps lower because of a fundamental development, do not get caught up in the emotion of thinking how rich you are going to be. Instead know that *smart money covers on the bad news.* When widely anticipated news is released and the stock drops sharply, who is left to sell? – the "dumbest money"/most stubborn players, whose stock is forced upon the market in frustration when bad news is released.

It is true that news events often lead to continued moves, but it is prudent to cover a portion of your trade when the emotional crowd rushes for the exit. Any remaining position should be managed aggressively to ensure that large accrued profits are not allowed to evaporate. Remember that *"bad news often comes out at bottoms."*

Stage 1- Exit. As we know, a downtrend will correct in one of two ways. If the stock violates the previous lower high on the 10-minute timeframe, the short-term trend becomes invalidated; this is my cue to exit any remaining short shares.

The other way stocks correct is through time. A short-term time correction often will often be resolved in the direction of the primary trend, but when the 10-minute timeframe shows the first signs of indecision (short-term moving average crossing above intermediate-term moving average), I cover any remaining shares of the stock. A short-term Stage 1 does not always lead to a short term Stage 2 advance; however it does signal a period where the rate of change has lost momentum and it is unlikely for the stock to continue lower in the short term. As a momentum trader, this is where I lose interest in any further participation in the stock.

Stage 2- Avoid. When the short-term trend of the stock shows higher highs and higher lows, the short-term trend is higher, and there is no reason to be short.   When the longer-term trend is lower and the short-term trend is higher, the trends of the varying timeframes are showing directional conflict and the stock should be left alone. A short-term Stage 2 in a primary Stage 4 stock should be avoided -- do not consider selling the stock until after the short-term strength has run its course, the stock experiences distribution and renews its decline.   While it is likely that the stock will continue lower again, early entries can subject you to large losses, and your goal is always to be in a position of strength.   Fighting even a two- to three-day trend exposes your equity to unnecessary risk.

Below is another example of trend alignment studied on three timeframes for a short sale.

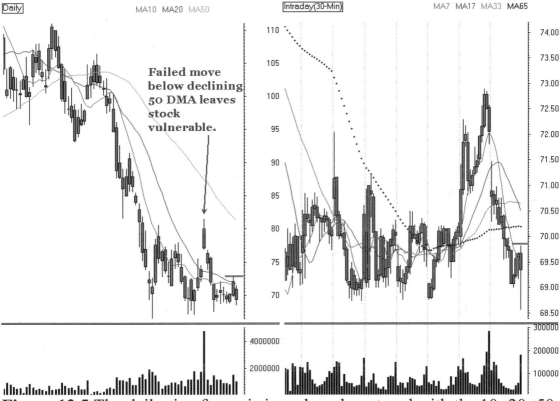

Figure 13.5 The daily timeframe is in a clear downtrend with the 10<20<50. The recent rally attempt below the declining 50-day moving average is shown in more detail on the hourly timeframe. This is a good example of the phrase "from failed moves come fast moves." A break below the lows near 68.75 put the stock in a position of new lows. In this case, the worst-

case stop would probably go just above the 5-day moving average that is just starting to decline again. RealTick by Townsend Analytics.

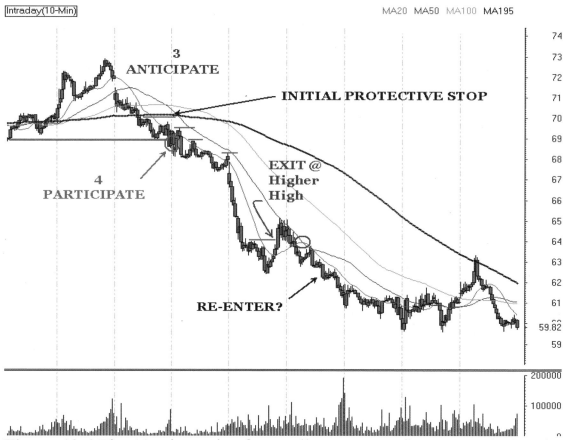

Figure 13.6 The 10-minute timeframe allows us to refine our analysis. The proper entry is made as the stock breaks support and trades to a lower low. The initial stop should be placed just above the most recent lower high, which is also the location of the declining 195 period (5-day) moving average near 70.00. As the stock creates further lower lows, the stop should be trailed down above the successively lower highs. After a slow start, the selling increased dramatically and the stop would have been triggered near 64.00. As the stock continued lower, you can see that there is no perfect technique. *Only liars buy the exact low, focus on making smart trading decisions, not on picking highs and lows.* RealTick by Townsend Analytics.

CHAPTER 14
NEWS: PERCEPTION IS REALITY

You may be wondering what a chapter on news is doing in a book about technical analysis. A technical purist would take a closed-minded approach, indicating that "fundamentals don't matter because the chart tells all." Just as many fundamentally oriented managers express their perceived disdain for technical analysis ("Reading charts is like reading tea leaves.").

The practical truth is that participants place their trades based on analysis of both fundamentals *and* technicals, and to completely ignore either is foolish. Don't start thinking that I'm talking out of both sides of my mouth here – 95 percent of this book is dedicated to technical analysis, and the other five percent to this chapter. *All of my timing decisions are based on price, not news or fundamentals.*

Human nature is to ask questions. People want to know the "why" of those things they don't understand right away. The markets are no different. All of us try to assign order to chaos, and crowd behavior in reaction to news frequently is very chaotic. We often do this instead of focusing on why a stock *has already* moved.

Personally, I want to know why people buy stocks in much more general terms. More importantly, though, I want to anticipate what their *next* move might be, when it may occur, how much risk to take and how much can I make if my analysis is correct.

In the market, the answer to why isn't always easy to understand. Fortunately for traders, it doesn't always matter. Interpreting news and committing capital based on our views of those events is very one-dimensional, just as monitoring the actions of just one participant is one-dimensional. *But correctly interpreting human nature and crowd behavior is really what understanding technical analysis is all about.* What causes one participant to buy or sell has very little significance beyond a couple of days.

It has been shown over and over again that no one is bigger than the markets -- remember Long Term Capital Management, Amaranth Partners, Bear Stearns and some of the other large "smart money" participants who went down in flames? If a very large participant attempts to move a stock – or even the market -- it can be accomplished for short periods of time, but it is very risky because it puts that institution in a large and likely difficult-to-liquidate position if the market moves against them quickly. Without proper risk controls in place, even the largest market participants can be forced out of business. Incidentally, many of the stocks you will trade successfully with a short-term timeframe are the recipient of a participant attempting to move prices in a particular direction.

Fundamentals Do Make Market Participants React

Fundamentals do matter because they are often the catalyst that causes a large group of participants to take buy or sell actions. There are many technical traders who buy breakouts or sell a stock short as it breaks below support. On a larger scale, there are more participants who buy and sell stocks based on their perceptions of a company or its products.

News releases are the biggest catalysts for participants to reevaluate their thinking about a company and make position adjustments based on expectations and ideas of value gained from the new information. *News triggers emotion, and that emotion triggers actions that can be measured on price charts.*

In college we are taught to evaluate a company based on its fundamentals, while technical study is given almost no attention. I learned a great deal in business school, but very little of it has helped me to become a good trader. What *has* helped me attain trading success with fundamental information is an understanding of when it makes sense to pay attention to these catalysts as it gives me insight into the psychology of the fundamental crowd.

I do believe that "the market knows all" and also that "news and surprises tend to follow the direction of the primary trend." One of the principles of technical analysis is that the market discounts the past and anticipates the future. Whether it is anticipating where the economy will be in six to twelve months or the lifecycle of a business product, *the smart money attempts to position its holdings to take advantage of emotional responders to the news when it is released.* Financial analysis is big business, and institutions pay millions of dollars per year to access information based on in-depth analysis of what the future may hold for the economy, a market sector or an individual stock – and for good reason. It is the goal of an institution to accumulate shares before the "good news" is known to the majority of

130

participants so they can be in a position to sell shares as price and volume expand.

When positive news is released, it is usually the public who buys from professionals. When negative news is released the coin flips, and professionals are often the buyers from the emotional public. The smart money buys temporary setbacks in a bull market and sells their long positions on short-term rallies in a bear market. It is common for strong markets to ignore negative news ("climb a wall of worry"), while weak markets react quickly and severely. Bear markets tend to ignore positive news and slide down a "slope of hope" or react with limited enthusiasm.

Today's near-instant dissemination of information can be an undisciplined trader's worst nightmare. Inexperienced and uneducated market participants -- the "dumb money" -- are more likely to be motivated by news headlines, chat room gossip, etc., and the market dutifully punishes their lack of thoughtful preparation with losses. *Simply put, professionals anticipate while amateurs react.*

Interpreting the News
As discussed, emotions are the enemy in trading, and it is easy to get caught up in the hype of a news story whether it appears to be bullish or bearish. Slowing down and introspectively answering questions about a news release can help keep you from making a knee-jerk reactionary buy or sell.

- Does it look like the information was "priced into the market" prior to the release? If the stock made a significant move in the days before the news report, there is a good chance that the move will fail, as the participants who anticipated the event will take advantage of news hype to liquidate their position and thereby extinguish the trend.

- Is it even news? There are times when smaller companies will "repackage" a news release in order to get more attention than the first time it was released. Small companies also will try to associate themselves with larger companies in an attempt to make their company appear more legitimate and stir up an emotional response from overly optimistic participants. Unfortunately for trusting buyers, news releases are sometimes used to generate public interest in a situation that may not be as optimistic as it appears.

- Is there a pattern to how the stock has acted when similar news was released? A good example of this would be quarterly earnings reports.

Answering these and similar questions allows you to slow your reaction to news headlines and think a situation through before deciding to commit your capital to a trade. *You should be more interested in understanding the psychology of participants and what motivates them to buy or sell than knowing the fundamentals of a business.*

How Is the Market Reacting?

Once the news (for the economy or a stock) has been released, traders should be less interested in interpreting the news itself and focus more on how the market reacts to it. With that in hand, it's easier to either ignore the news and focus solely on price action or find a low-risk way to exploit any subsequent movements.

Treat price reactions cautiously. Let the market first absorb the short-term emotional response, and then focus on the unfolding market action to determine if there will be a lasting impact that can be exploited in a low- risk manner. Some of the common actions following a news release are:

- The reaction can *fizzle out* (Figure 14.1), and the stock enters a period of inactivity (avoid these stocks).

- Significant news can *create a new trending environment.* If a stock breaks out of a longer-term consolidation after a news release, there is a high likelihood that the new trend will be able to sustain the move, particularly if the breakout is accompanied by a surge in trading volume. (Figure 14.2)

- When a stock is already in an established trend, news releases will often motivate enough participants to take action and *accelerate an existing trend.*

- Occasionally a true surprise catches a large group of participants off guard, and sentiment changes so drastically that the stock may *reverse the prevailing trend.*

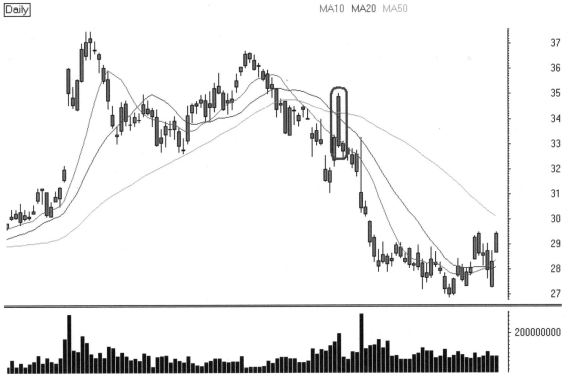

Figure 14.1 After gapping higher in response to earnings, the sellers were able to push the stock back below the declining 50-day moving average. Failure to hold the initial gains forced more emotional sellers to the market, and it caved in. RealTick by Townsend Analytics.

Below are a few of the potential big catalysts of which you should always be aware.

Earnings

Earnings reports are one of the biggest catalysts for volatility in an individual stock, so be aware of the date earnings are due for the stocks you choose to trade. Every three months publicly traded corporations are required to compile their financial results and provide the public with information about their current financial condition. Most corporations prepare these results at the end of a calendar quarter. It usually takes one to six weeks for corporations to report results to the public, and the time it takes for the majority of companies to report is known as earnings season.

Earnings season actually begins with "earnings warnings" about two to three weeks before the actual results are publicly released. As a company realizes that their results might fall short of what they previously indicated, they try to get the news out to the market quickly by issuing a "warning." These warnings take many participants off guard and are dealt with quickly and often severely as shareholders rush for the exits all at once. While the earnings warning only speeds up the markets' reaction to the news, it is a tradition on Wall Street that helps the reporting company to be "trusted" in bad times. It also helps the time it takes for the stock to recover from such a violation.

For an individual stock, the earnings release is a catalyst that causes a large group of participants to reevaluate their perception of value (Figure 14.2). Earnings news can have a catastrophic effect on the price of a stock, or it can send a stock soaring, which makes trading stocks during earnings season more volatile than other times of the year. While it is true that news and surprises tend to follow the direction of the trend, there are the occasional land mines in the market that can be avoided by reducing exposure before such an important event. The most obvious thing to do is to find out when a company is due to report earnings and then make sure that you are not holding a stock position ahead of the report.

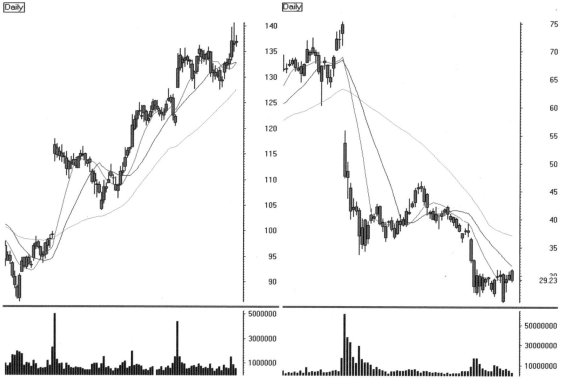

Figure 14.2 Earnings reports are one of the primary catalysts for fundamental investors to re-evaluate their idea of value. The initial earnings reactions often turn into powerful, long-lasting trends. RealTick by Townsend Analytics.

On a macro scale, there are times when economic report releases can have a large impact on asset pricing, and you want to be aware of some of the common reports. Your goal as a trader should not be to be an expert at interpreting every economic number that comes out; leave that for the economists. Your job is to interpret the reaction to the catalyst and then formulate a low-risk strategy based on how the market reacts based on predetermined technical levels.

U.S Government Economic Reports

These numbers are released to the public at 8:30 a.m. ET and are broken down by government agency. Economic reports also can cause emotional trading that, in turn, produces a knee-jerk reaction in the futures markets that can influence the regular equities session.

Department of Labor:

Employment Situation
Consumer Price Index
Producer Price Index
Import and Export Price Indices
Productivity and Cost Index

Bureau of Economic Analysis:

Gross Domestic Product
Trade Balance
Current Account Balance
Personal Income
Personal Consumption Expenditure

Federal Reserve Policy Meetings and Changes

The Federal Reserve Open Market Committee (FOMC) holds eight regularly scheduled meetings each year, with occasional "emergency meetings" as necessary. The minutes for these meetings are released three weeks after the date of the policy decision. While the impact of the actual meeting is most widely anticipated, and causes the most dramatic shifts in market pricing, the release of the minutes can also motivate participants to reallocate funds based on the details revealed from the previous meeting.

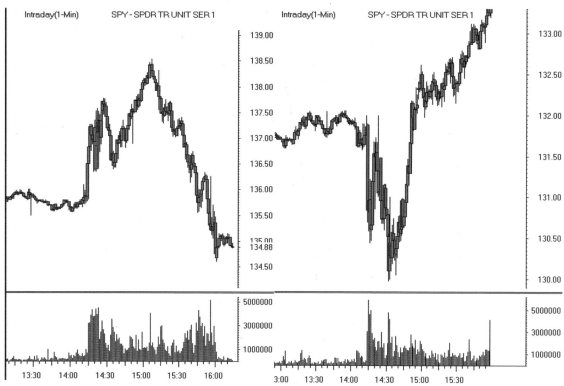

Figure 14.3 The FOMC typically announces any change to monetary policy at 2:15 p.m. Eastern. Trading in the markets tends to be extremely volatile just after the announcement is made. RealTick by Townsend Analytics.

Other potential market moving news and events specific to individual stocks to be aware of include:

- Annual meetings
- Stock splits
- Share buyback programs
- Analyst revisions
- Conferences
- FDA reports
- Insider transactions

During periods of heightened uncertainty, markets become more volatile as emotional participants read news reports in search of clarity where none may actually exist. Learn to focus on price action, and if there is no price clarity, cash is your best position until a low-risk action point reveals itself.

And don't confuse your opinion of a good company with a good stock. Good stocks move in the direction of your trades. There are no good companies, only good trades. *Think like a fundamentalist, and trade like a technician.* It can be comforting to know why others may be interested in a stock, but price confirmation is a must before getting involved, no matter how bullish or bearish the news may seem. Also note that in their constant need to try to satisfy for viewers why a movement occurred, the media becomes obsessed with the explaining the "reasons" for market activity. Don't become obsessed with the media, however. It takes away from the time you have to rationally plan your next move.

Our job as traders is to objectively observe the supply and demand imbalances in the issues we are trading while we take advantage of the trends that are created by these imbalances. Leave the reasons for the journalists and academics to debate while we go about our business of harvesting profits from the markets. Listen to the market!

CHAPTER 15
THE SHORT SQUEEZE

Selling short stocks in downtrends is an essential skill and often quite a lucrative strategy. As emphasized in Chapter 13 on short selling, if you are a professional trader, you need to be willing to sell short at times when the market dictates. Though short selling has some special cautions, you are limiting your trading opportunities if you ignore the short side of the market.

The best times to go short are when the market is in an overall Stage 4 decline, when the industry in which your stock is classified is in decline and the stock is also showing weakness. Of course, there will also be excellent opportunities to profit from short sales when a stock is trading lower without the sector or market declining as well. Unless you want to become the victim of a short squeeze, do not sell short when you think a stock "is up too much," the "P/E is too high" or any other subjective reason.

When a stock is sold short, remember that sellers represent future demand for the stock because they must repurchase shares they sold short at some future date either to close out a winning trade or to minimize their losses. The appeal of selling short is easy to understand because stocks can drop much faster and sharper than they rise. The reason is simple: Fear is a stronger motivator to take action to buy back a losing short or sell a losing long than greed is to initiate a position.

As with any strategy that is a straight directional bet, there are risks involved with selling short. The biggest risk to a short seller is that the stock price rises instead of drops. A rising share price in a heavily shorted stock can often lead to dramatic upward movement as losses mount in the accounts of those who are short as they attempt to minimize their losses by buying the stock back.

The main motivation to buy back the stock is *the fear of unlimited losses.* When you buy a stock at $20/share, your maximum loss is $20.00/share. But when you sell a stock short at $20, the potential for losses is, in theory, unlimited. The stock may rise to 40, a 100-percent loss, or it could just as easily climb to higher levels. It is the fear of such an advance that can make for an explosive upside move in a heavily shorted stock. *The phenomenon of a rapidly rising stock with a large short interest is known as a short squeeze.*

If you have ever been short a stock that is moving higher, you understand the fear that higher prices elicit from a trapped short seller. If you find yourself in this situation, the best bet is to put your emotions aside, buy the stock back, take your loss and repeat your vow never to trade against the trend again. The unemotional willingness to cut losses quickly is the sign of a true professional. It always boggles my mind to see a stock in a clear uptrend with a large short position that was established at lower prices. What is the logic of stepping in front of strong directional momentum in hopes of catching the ultimate top? Instead, why not safely wait for a downtrend to *fully reveal itself* before initiating a short position?

The Short Interest Ratio

Before exploring the actual dynamics of a short squeeze, let's cover some key terminology and learn how to analyze short interest data. The Short Interest Ratio (SIR), or days to cover, is the number of shares sold short (short interest) for a particular stock, divided by its average daily volume over the previous two weeks. The SIR is interpreted as the number of days it would theoretically take to cover (buy back) the shares sold short based on the average daily volume. I use the term "theoretically" because, in reality, the shorts would not be the only participants in the market. As a result, it normally takes longer to liquidate (buy back) these short positions. The higher the SIR, the more difficult it is for shorts to cover as their buying will create higher prices, thus sabotaging their own positions.

Examples of how SIR plays out mathematically:

- If the stock had a short position of 4,800,000 shares and an average daily volume of 800,000, the SIR would be 6.0. This means it would take six full days of average daily volume for the short sellers to cover their bearish bets.

- If the same stock traded an average of 2.4 million shares per day, the short interest for the stock would be 2.0, or two days to repurchase.

- Using the same stock, but with average daily volume of just 200,000 shares, the SIR would then be 24, meaning it would take 24 days of buying to cover the positions.

From a "trapped" short's standpoint, the lower the SIR, the better. However, from a contrarian standpoint, a higher SIR is desirable because it is more difficult to cover the position; thus, the resulting buys would have the potential to create significant upside momentum.

It is important to note that a large outstanding short position or short interest ratio by itself is not a reason for buying a stock in anticipation of a short squeeze. The informed trader will find an edge when there is a preponderance of indicators leading to a price advance. Nonetheless, it is an excellent gauge of potential demand for a stock which should be a part of every trader's arsenal.

Short sellers who initiate large positions against a stock typically are sophisticated speculators who have done extensive research on their targeted company and are often right. Many times those who sell short have the right idea fundamentally, but their timing is off. The correct time to sell a stock short is when it is either in or entering a downtrend. When a short position is initiated in a stock that is trending higher, there is real potential for losses to spiral out of control for the shorts.

When Does a Short Squeeze Occur?

A short squeeze develops when those who sold short the stock, expecting it to decline in price, change their minds about the trade and attempt to cover their position before the market advances and large losses accumulate.

Short squeezes often occur because of a news event that changes investor perception on the worth of a particular company. A short squeeze also can be created by long holders of the stock attempting to push the price higher to tap into the emotional buying that trapped short sellers can provide.

If you have ever been short an advancing stock, chances are there was a point at which you became afraid to continue holding that position. To eliminate the mounting losses and the emotional trauma of holding a big loser, you became a panicky buyer. This is not uncommon. It is this buying that makes the stock advance at a rapid pace as pressure of holding a losing position mounts, and the short seller gets "squeezed."

There are times when short sellers find themselves in a position of being forced by their brokerage firm to repurchase shares that have been sold short. There are two reasons for "forced buy-ins." The first is from margin calls. When losses in a short position have gone so far against a customer that their equity levels fall below exchange requirements, the brokerage firm is required by regulatory bodies – the SEC, NASD, etc. – to demand the customer either to deposit more margin money or buy back the shares. Never allow yourself to be in the position of a margin call whether you are trading long or short positions. If you ever receive a margin call on a long or short position, it means you need to work on money management.

The other reason for a forced buy-in of a short position comes when the shares shorted are no longer available to be borrowed against. When long holders of the stock who have allowed shares to be borrowed for a short position liquidate their holdings, short sellers who have borrowed those shares are left with an illegal "naked" position. When this occurs, it is the responsibility of the brokerage firm to demand that short sellers either find other shares to borrow, or force customers to buy back the stock. If the short seller cannot locate other shares to borrow, the short seller is required by securities regulations to repurchase shares or the brokerage firm will do it for them.

There is also a more sinister way in which the short sellers can be targeted for a squeeze with a forced buy-in. If large long holders wish to inflict maximum damage on short sellers, they will allow their stock to be borrowed until a time where the buyers have taken control of the trend. If an institution that is long (let's say one million shares) of stock suddenly demands that the shares loaned out be delivered back to that firm, the borrowers are stuck looking for new shares to borrow. Or they must cover the short position by repurchasing the shares they are short. Either way, it's a difficult situation. This is particularly effective at putting pressure on shorts because of its cold-hearted implementation. In effect, the long holder set the shorts up to be squeezed.

Loaning shares to be shorted is a source of revenue for some brokerage firms that can charge customers substantial fees for access to long positions in highly demanded stocks. Most investors purchase stocks "in street name," which means that the brokerage firm holds the shares. If shares are purchased in a margin account, it allows the brokerage firm to "hypothecate," (lend out) these shares to other customers who may want to establish a short position.

An alternative is to purchase shares and request that an actual stock certificate is issued, but this is rarely done. It is possible to request shares to be held in street name but not be allowed to be borrowed for short positions.

If you open a "cash account" without margin capability (and therefore a hypothecation agreement), your shares will not be available to be borrowed.

Another way to prevent your long position from being borrowed is to enter a "good-until-cancelled" (GTC) sell order on the stock at a price you believe has little chance of being transacted. For instance, if your stock is trading at $20, you may enter a GTC order to sell the shares at $50. Because you have a pending order to liquidate your long position, the brokerage firm cannot lend out the shares in your account.

Short Squeeze Play #1

I consider there to be two different types of short squeeze plays. The first is what I call a **knee-jerk emotional short squeeze** (Figure 15.2). This squeeze occurs in a declining stock with a large short position. *When a stock in an established Stage 4 decline is accompanied by a large short position, short sellers are in control of the trend,* and their accumulated profits make them less likely to panic and buy at the first signs of strength. Keep in mind that short sellers can be some of the sharpest minds on the planet, and they may be right. When prices are declining, they can dig their heels in, staying short until, in the most severe down market, the stock becomes delisted if the company declares bankruptcy.

Stage 4 stocks can experience quick and large rallies, but those short-term bursts higher typically will fail as longer-term selling pressure is too strong to overcome. It is common to see an emotional burst of buying by shorts after a stock has sold off hard for a week or more. These stocks exhaust all sellers from the market after a relentless fearful selling campaign. In addition, declining prices attract momentum short sellers who pile on extra shares of short stock near a short-term low, their confidence buoyed by short-term profits. A simple absence of further supply will push shorts to begin to cover their shares, but with limited supply their buying forces the stock higher. The initial strength brought on by these short sellers then attracts short-term sidelined cash to the stock in search of quick long-side profits in the longer-term downtrend. As short and long traders compete for limited supply of shares, it can send the prices quickly higher.

Indeed trading these short-term rallies can result in great short-term trading gains, but because the dominant trend of the longer timeframe is lower, they are very risky trades. They are best left to the most risk-tolerant traders who specialize in the shortest timeframes. The best course of action is to stay with the primary trend rather than charter these risky waters.

Getting a Broader Sense of Short Action

It is useful to know that when a stock is sold short, exchanges mandate the brokerage firms to record it. Twice each month, the firms tally all short sales not covered by their customers and send the data to the various exchanges. The exchanges then combine the firm data and publicly disseminate the information the on the 15th and last calendar day of each month. Take a look at Figure 15.1 below to get a sense of the data. My favorite free site for finding short interest data is www.nasdaq.com

	Date	Short Interest	Avg Volume	S.I.R.	VWAP
9	2/29	21,275,047	2,651,156	8.02	17.68
8	2/15	19,867,817	2,559,249	7.76	18.52
7	1/31	17,871,618	4,345,058	4.11	20.91
6	1/15	19,007,950	2,866,400	6.63	23.36
5	12/31	19,276,055	1,492,816	12.91	27.24
4	12/14	17,035,558	1,886,753	9.02	29.9
3	11/30	17,776,362	2,426,715	7.32	29.36
2	11/15	13,937,413	1,852,338	7.52	32.9
1	10/31	12,091,492	1,660,065	7.28	34.88
	10/15	11,670,909	1,195,727	9.76	

Figure 15.1 Short interest data table. The numbers (9-1) in the left-hand column provide a visual reference (on Figure 15.2 below) of when the short sellers added shares.

1- **Date:** Bi-monthly data date

2- **Short Interest:** Total number of shares sold short but not covered

3- **AverageVolume:** Average number of shares traded per day over 2 weeks (rolling)

4- **Short Interest Ratio** (also referred to as Days to Cover): The number of days it would take short sellers to cover their bearish positions, it is calculated by dividing the short interest by the average daily share volume of the previous 2 weeks.

5-   **Volume Weighted Average Price (VWAP):** Average price at which the stock traded during the prior period, it offers an idea of the average price at which short sellers may be involved. (I have added the VWAP info to this table as I refer to it often; at www.alphatrends.net.)

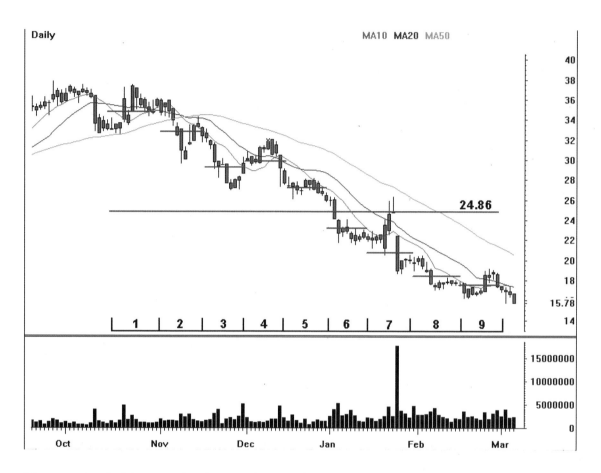

Figure 15.2 The stock above shows the stock whose data is represented in Figure 15.1. RealTick by Townsend Analytics.

Note that as the stock above (Figure 15.2) broke down, the short sellers became more aggressive, raising their bet against the stock from 11.6 million shares to 21.2 million (Figure 15.1). During period 7 on the chart you can see that the large volatility motivated shorts to cover approximately 1.2 million shares. As the stock continued lower, the shorts added even more shares.

Short Squeeze Play #2

A second short squeeze is one I call a ***structural short squeeze***. It occurs when an uptrending stock has a large short position which was initiated at lower levels.

By combining the information from the short interest tables (Figure 15.3) and the price chart (Figure 15.4) below, you can determine the approximate level where the majority of the outstanding short positions were initiated. *Using this information to recognize the approximate price at which a large short position begins to lose money lets you hone in on stocks that may be poised for a squeeze.* If the majority of short positions were initiated at lower levels, the growing losses in a rising stock motivate short sellers to reconsider their positions and repurchase the stock. The short covering becomes an additional source of demand which adds further pressure to the average short seller. This type of squeeze setup can lead to substantial moves higher as it is based on a large group of participants being wrong in a stock with upward momentum.

	Date	Short Interest	Avg Volume	S.I.R.	VWAP
10	2/15	7,694,606	1,281,125	6.00	40.64
9	1/31	6,396,162	1,509,795	4.23	42.85
8	1/15	6,359,908	1,439,337	4.41	40.53
7	12/31	4,490,911	854,718	5.25	43.18
6	12/14	4,565,105	1,301,907	3.50	42.21
5	11/30	4,252,342	959,083	4.43	41.93
4	11/15	4,915,648	800,581	6.14	43.34
3	10/31	4,551,506	1,294,847	3.51	45.02
2	10/15	5,287,970	1,296,446	4.07	44.05
1	9/28	4,468,885	1,425,010	3.13	40.85
	9/14	6,698,123	2,412,571	2.36	

Figure 15.3 The table above should be viewed with the chart in Figure 15.4.

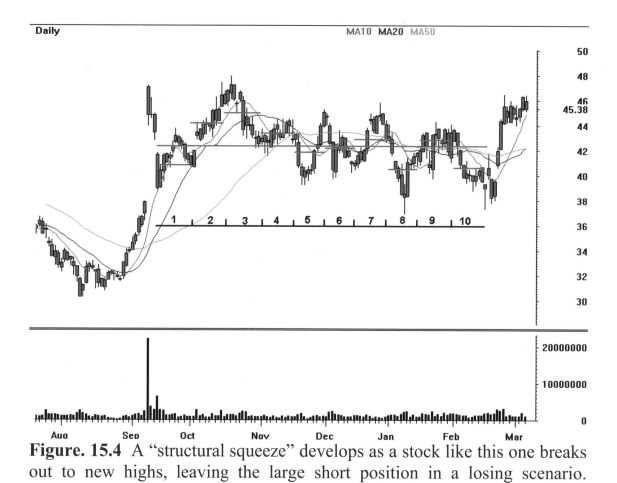

Figure. 15.4 A "structural squeeze" develops as a stock like this one breaks out to new highs, leaving the large short position in a losing scenario. RealTick by Townsend Analytics.

The stock in Figure 15.4 represents what looks like an excellent candidate for a structural short squeeze. The VWAP for the entire period 1-10 was 42.37 (long horizontal blue line), which means that at the current price the average short seller was down approximately $3.00/share. A closer examination of the short interest shows those who initiated a position in period 8 (12/31 to 1/15 represented by a shorter blue horizontal line) sold short just less than two million shares at an average price of 40.53. With the stock nearing highs and the 10-, 20- and 50-day moving averages all advancing, I would be nervous if I was short this stock.

Finally, here are some general points to help you determine which stocks may become squeeze candidates:

1- **Uptrend on the daily timeframe.** At a minimum, the stock must be above the rising 50-day moving average. Stocks at or near all-time highs are best because there is no real motivated source of supply when all the longs are in a winning position. *If the stock is in a* *downtrend, it is not a good squeeze candidate, as short sellers are in control and have no reason for aggressive repurchases.*

2- **Absence of any hedging vehicles.** Some common ways for short sellers to hedge bearish bets are with options, a different class of common stock, warrants, convertibles, preferred stock or any other hedge products. If there is an inability to hedge short exposure, it will leave the short seller in a more vulnerable position.

3- **Short interest** should be high relative to average volume; the higher the SIR, the greater the difficulty short sellers will have in the repurchase of their shares, thus resulting in higher prices.

4- **Level of potential squeeze**. Check to see approximate level at which the majority of shorts were initiated; this can be approximated with the Volume Weighted Average Pricing (VWAP) tool. When the stock rises above this level, the average short seller is losing money; that makes the shorts vulnerable to a squeeze.

Stocks with double sources of demand (longs and shorts) and tight supply (especially if the stock is at an all-time high) can lead to excellent trending opportunities. Short sellers are usually very savvy speculators. However, like any group of market participants, they aren't always right. When shorts are wrong about the direction of a stock, their move to cover can lead to some excellent short-term profits for traders who are able to recognize the squeeze situation developing.

CHAPTER 16
RISK MANAGEMENT

The goal of all trading and investing is to make money without taking uncomfortable levels of risk. No matter how well you have researched your market opportunities, what you know/think you know, or how recent price action may reinforce your reasons for entering a trade, risk is your constant companion. It can be your best friend if you give it the respect it's due or your worst enemy if you do not.

Thus, your most important job is that of a risk manager. Although all of us at least theoretically have control over risk by adjusting share size, maintaining realistic expectations and making proper timing decisions, the market is the real master. That's precisely why you must remain objective to interpret its message and be prepared to react quickly and unemotionally to all possible outcomes *before* initiating a position. One of the biggest distinctions between professional traders and those who treat trading as a hobby is the ability to prepare for any outcome – win, lose or draw – and to consider in advance where they will call it quits on losing positions. To ignore this lesson will have dire consequences. The market will either eat you alive quickly or take little bites out of you over time to punish you for not knowing who is king.

For a professional, the category in which you'd eventually like to include yourself, taking losses is an everyday part of the business. What separates the professionals from the amateurs is how those losses are handled. Professionals always have a backup plan in mind for the "what ifs." Your ability to identify and then remove emotions from entries and exits frees you from the paralyzing insecurities which plague so many struggling traders.

There are five possible outcomes of a trade – a large winner, a small winner, a breakeven trade, a small loss or a large loss. It is the large losses that must be avoided at all cost.

When large losses occur, the most common reasons are trading too large of a share size relative to overall equity, ego-driven decision-making, or an adverse fundamental development. There is also the possibility of losing capital by taking too many small losses; this is also known as "death by 1,000 paper cuts." In other words, you can indeed make money on more than 50 percent of your trades but still go broke either with small losses or large losses if your profits aren't allowed to run long enough to swallow up the smaller losers.

Taking losses stinks. I have heard that you have to learn to "love your losers." Though I have never loved a loser, I have learned a great deal from my losing trades and have been happy to take a small loss and then be vindicated by watching a stock completely implode after I have exited. I take some solace in knowing that my discipline saved me from potential disaster.

Types of Risk

Price. Price, of course, is the risk that is most easily quantified. Prior to initiating a trade, it is critical to establish a theoretical risk/reward ratio – the expected amount of risk you are willing to take in relation to the projected profit on your investment.

I personally use a generally accepted 1:3 risk/reward as my guide, which means I am willing to risk $1.00 for an expected gain of at least $3.00. But to keep your expectations realistic, you must base these decisions on supply/demand dynamics and locations of most recent support and resistance levels on the timeframe you are trading.

Stop placement and potential target levels should be based on what you *actually see* on the chart, not on random percentages or dollar amounts. The concept of risk/reward sounds good, but it is only based on our *subjective market assumptions*. Just because you want a 1:3 risk/reward scenario to play out for a potential trade setup does not mean the market will agree with your analysis. It really doesn't give a tinker's damn what you believe.

A risk/reward ratio takes into consideration the expected entry price, where the initial protective stop will be placed and where the stock is expected to encounter support or resistance that may slow it down. This is a price objective.

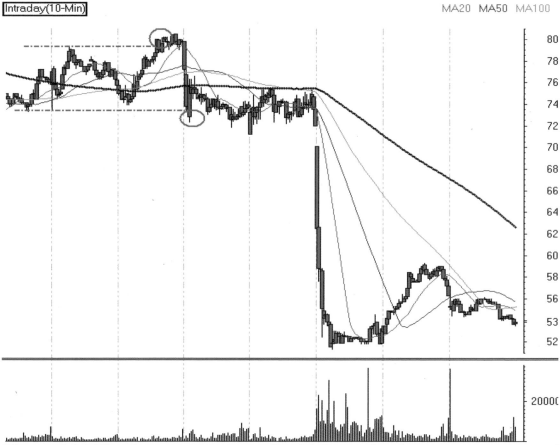

Figure 16.1 The three components of a risk/reward ratio are; entry, stop and profit objective. Using a 10-minute timeframe, we can establish the entry and initial stop levels. The approximation of a price objective comes from analyzing a longer timeframe.   RealTick by Townsend Analytics.

Market Risk. As a trader, you need to assess current risk levels in the market each day. Participants most certainly change their focus, and you must be especially cognizant of the heightened overall risk environment resulting from these changes. Common times of heightened risk include, but are not limited to; earnings season each quarter, economic report releases, Federal Reserve meetings, and others. During these times participants can still find good, profitable setups in the market, but they should be traded less aggressively (in share size) than during more "normal" conditions. Varying your position size is the easiest way to deal with changing risk levels.

Time. In addition to price-based risk, the markets present time-based risk. Tying up your capital in a non-performing asset is a waste of time when you could be in something that's performing better.

A professional approach to handling risk must include not just price-based stops, but also time-based stops. If the anticipated market activity has not occurred within a specific amount of time, then liquidate most, if not all, of your position. How long should a stock be given to perform before a time stop is executed? There are no hard and fast rules here, but for a day trade, it does necessitate exiting before the market session is completed. For other trades, the length of a time stop will be influenced by your personal objectives, knowledge of the situation, capital availability, mental concentration, position size and opportunity cost.

By the way, the risks of holding a stock position overnight have received an unfair amount of attention. Granted, things can go wrong overnight, but a little common sense can keep you from experiencing catastrophic losses. And it's a double-edged sword. Holding a winner overnight can give you an opportunity to cash in on continued profits at the expense of those who miss out on the previous day's action and then chase a stock on the open. For short-term traders, though, only hold stocks overnight where you already have a profit. If you have a losing position, liquidate it by the end of the day, and start fresh the next morning.

If you are unaccustomed to holding a position overnight, ease into it by selling the majority of your shares and holding 50 percent or even just 25 percent of your position overnight until you get used to it. Naturally, there are times when holding even what appears to be an excellent trending stock overnight presents a larger risk. Some of those potential signposts can be clearly identified, including earnings or economic reports, or a stock which is nearing a key level of support or resistance which leaves limited potential for further profits.

What Percentage Winners?
It is important for you to understand that making money in the market isn't about being right a specified percentage of the time. It's more about how much you make when you are right compared to how much you lose when you are wrong. I have had extremely profitable months when my winning ratio was just 45 percent. A 45-percent winning ratio sounds terrible, but in active trading a number of very small losers which are exited quickly and then "absorbed" by a handful of trades closed out with large gains can mean a terrific month. This simply entails holding your winners and cutting your losers quickly.

Know, too, that your mindset on losses will go a long way in determining your emotional state. There are often trades where you lose money but do so in a disciplined way before the stock position turns into a disaster; I look at these small losers as successful trades. The success is obviously not measured in dollars and cents, but instead in your ability to manage risk smartly on your terms based on a predefined assessment of risk.

Holding winners and cutting losers is the basic theory behind money management. Why then is it one of the biggest areas of downfall for market participants? The simple reason is ego. Traders who brag about their 80 percent or higher win/loss ratios may still manage to lose money on balance because these high percentages are achieved by doing the exact *opposite* of what is right – selling winners very quickly and holding on to losers, allowing those losses to grow while waiting for them in vain to come back to profit territory.

Trade date: ◄ 1/1 ► SELECT DATE

Trade date: ◄ 1/21 ► SELECT DATE SUBMIT

Long vs Short	Trades	Gains	Losses	P/L	Best	Worst	% Gainers	Average Trade
Long	256	133	123	4,525.08	825.36	-799.90	52.0%	17.68
Short	101	57	44	1,497.71	895.66	-974.20	56.4%	14.83
Long vs Short Net								

Shares Traded	Trades	Gains	Losses	P/L	Best	Worst	% Gainers	Average Trade
Less than 200	56	32	24	143.03	558.00	-799.90	57.1%	1.49
201 - 500	173	94	79	2,436.60	895.66	-974.20	54.3%	3.24
501 - 750	7	6	1	600.23	374.06	-63.36	85.7%	17.65
751 - 1000	107	50	57	533.37	759.12	-439.04	46.7%	0.94
Greater than 1000	14	8	6	2,309.57	825.36	-294.10	57.1%	15.10

Share Price	Trades	Gains	Losses	P/L	Best	Worst	% Gainers	Average Trade
Less Than $10.00	9	6	3	937.72	434.64	-104.33	66.7%	7.69
$10.01 - $25	52	33	19	4,269.04	825.36	-260.09	63.5%	14.82
$25.01 - $50	48	30	18	1,564.06	405.46	-417.14	62.5%	6.09
$50.01 - $100	89	46	43	1,298.00	895.66	-372.49	51.7%	3.24
Greater than $100	159	75	84	-2,046.03	558.00	-974.20	47.2%	-3.82

Term of Trade	Trades	Gains	Losses	P/L	Best	Worst	% Gainers	Average Trade
Day Trade	350	189	161	6,393.34	895.66	-974.20	54.0%	18.27

Minutes in Day Trade	Trades	Gains	Losses	P/L	Best	Worst	% Gainers	Average Trade
0 - 5 minutes	168	99	69	3,873.90	533.90	-974.20	58.9%	23.06
6 - 15 minutes	99	47	52	1,847.94	895.66	-799.90	47.5%	18.67
16 - 30 minutes	44	22	22	-788.99	405.46	-417.14	50.0%	-17.93
31 - 60 minutes	23	13	10	415.35	394.72	-173.04	56.5%	18.06
61 - 120 minutes	11	5	6	342.33	427.86	-163.22	45.5%	31.12
More than 120 minutes	5	3	2	702.81	434.64	-63.04	60.0%	140.56

Figure 16.2 The "Trade Evaluator" report from www.terranovaonline.com allows you to study your trade data objectively. Notice the circled data fields where the winning percentage rate was less than 50%. In these three instances, the overall profitability was achieved by having larger winners than losers.

Winning percentages sound fantastic, but the only numbers that matter are the ones on your profit/loss statement. One of my golf partners said it best. "Brian," he said, "when you turn in your scorecard, they only ask how many, not how you did it."

Here is the basic math behind the reasoning that winners need to be held longer than losers!

If I lose:	I need to make:
10%	11%
20%	25%
50%	100%

Trade Size

Learn early on that position size should not be a constant in terms of shares traded, dollars committed to an idea, or percentages at risk. The first consideration for position size is determining if there is an acceptable perceived amount of reward present for the amount of risk you expect to take in the trade.

Coming up with a risk/reward ratio is done by determining entry level, where the initial stop should be placed, and the price area to which you expect the stock to travel if you are right. While no formula will take into consideration all of the relevant variables for determining position size, one place to begin is the maximum percentage of your overall trading capital you are willing to lose if you are wrong. A commonly used percentage is approximately one percent of trading capital. For a trading account with $100,000 in equity, for example, this would translate to maximum risk of $1,000. If you lose on your first trade, your equity is now $99,000, and you should not risk more than one percent of *that* capital, or $990. On the flip side, if you earn $10,000 on your first trade (thus giving you an account value of $110,000, with your next trade you could risk one percent of the new balance – or $1,100.

To be fair, know that this concept has some potential shortcomings, so a little bit of further drill down is necessary here. Let's use two examples assuming a starting account balance of $100,000.

Example one uses a stock at $50/share that typically trades 10 million shares/day. For this $50 stock, you have determined that a reasonable stop should be placed just below recent support at 49.25, which would be a risk of $0.75/share. You also determine that the potential price target for this trade would be 52.25, or $2.25/share. If the market agrees with your analysis, you stand to make $3.00 for every $1 you place at risk, an acceptable risk/reward. If you take your risk amount of 1,000 and divide it by .75, then an appropriate number of shares would be 1,333 shares (most traders would round this order off to 1,300 shares to avoid trading an odd lot). Based on an average volume of 10 million shares per day, this would be a reasonably sized position, as liquidity would not be a concern. But would you really want to commit 65% of your trading capital to just one idea?

But now let's add some variables. What if the company's main competitor, whose stock this one mirrors closely, is due to report earnings? How much impact would that have on your decision? Would you want to cut your share size in half due to this variable, or perhaps buy call options instead, which would put a strict limit on the amount of capital you could lose but might also minimize your upside? What if there was an important economic report due out the next morning or the Federal Reserve was planning a meeting to determine if there should be any change to monetary policy? You can see that using a simple position sizing formula definitely has its shortcomings.

For our second example, we'll use a stock priced at $2.50. Your analysis shows what looks like major support at $2.35 (just $0.15 away) and a potential price target near $3.00 (representing a gain of $0.65/share). Assuming $1,000 at risk, you would then be able to purchase 6,666 shares of this stock. Risking 15 cents to make 65 cents would be better than a 1:4 risk/reward ratio, and this certainly sounds better than the potential for the $50 stock. But, remember, there are variables to consider. What if the average volume for this stock was just 300,000 shares per day? Would you feel comfortable buying 6,000 shares? Well, do you have good discipline and order-entry skills? If not, it may be more difficult than you imagine to exit your position with a profit or a loss. For this stock, also add in the other variables from the previous example, or others, and see how complicated it can become to determine the optimal trade size each and every time you enter a position.

Of course, even if imperfect, a simple plan for trade size like this one is better than randomly buying 500 or 1,000 shares each time you enter the market. There are times when it pays to be more conservative or aggressive than what your "rules" may tell you, but in general my advice is to err on the side of being conservative. Occasionally the market will present you with the opportunity to "go for it," and those opportunities should only be seized if you possess the discipline for handling a larger trade. The most common mistake I see traders making, however, is trying to make up for a string of losses with one outsized bet in an attempt to put their account equity back to where they think it should be. It is extremely rare to actually yield a positive outcome in these cases, and even if there is, it just reinforces a negative behavior that will unrealistically boost your confidence and set you up for even bigger losses in the future.

As a general rule, you never want to risk more than one to two percent of your overall capital on any trade. Further, exposing more than 15 to 20 percent of your account equity to any one position can result in disastrous effects on your account balance if something unexpected goes wrong. Money management and position sizing are never a constant, as the many factors such as trader experience, liquidity of issue being traded, anticipated time horizon, volatility, time of day/season/year, market volatility, potential for a fundamental catalyst are all important considerations.

Just Do It!
Given our focus on ensuring that losses are cut to a minimum before the market spirals to create obscene losses, when it is time to sell, then sell! You need to have a "me-first" attitude when it comes time to exit a trade before someone else comes in and robs the market of the liquidity you need to exit gracefully. A common mistake is to wait for volume to show up before exiting a loser. If you fall into this common trap, you often will be too late because the volume is usually greatest *after* price has moved.

In trading, as in any risky activity, there are ways to add some safeguards. I used to fly hang gliders and was fully aware of the risks. I would not fly with questionable equipment, without a backup parachute or when the weather was sketchy. Other people did not take the same precautions, more or less throwing caution to the wind. The consequences were severe. The same is true in trading, where basic rules help control risk.

Managing Winners: No Complacency Allowed

It is often said that "winners take care of themselves," but that attitude of complacency is very dangerous. Winning positions need to be managed as aggressively as losers by locking in profits before the market takes them back. Managing winners is a fun job, but there is a fine balance between exiting a winning position too early and letting it turn into a problem.

My preferred style of exiting is to scale out incrementally with my first sale occurring as the stock makes its first thrust higher. Moving out of a small amount of the position with a small profit relieves some of the initial risk in the remaining shares and allows you to deal with the balance from a position of strength. Scaling out of a winning trade incrementally will keep you from realizing the absolute maximum profit on a trade, but to expect the max on every trade is unrealistic anyway. The fear of leaving money on the table keeps many inexperienced traders in positions well past the point where a professional takes profits. As the amateur sees his profits deteriorate, his mind fixates on getting back to the high equity point in his account. This mistake causes him to become paralyzed and ride the stock back down to a level where he actually experiences a loss on what was once a strong winner. Letting winners turn into losers is unacceptable, and the more seasoned traders don't do it.

Before we get to specific strategies, know that there is no single best way of exiting a position. We all have different objectives in terms of preferred trade timeframes, risk tolerances and account sizes, and we may also implement multiple strategies to fit our diversification and income-stream objectives. The objectives and methods of a day trader will be vastly different than that of a more patient individual who is comfortable holding a position for months at a time. We're all different.

In the following examples, we will refer to the long side of the market for the sake of simplicity. However, the principles are just as valid on the short side simply by reversing the rules.

It is often said that entering a stock is easy, but knowing when to sell (or cover a short) is what separates the best traders from those who just scrape by. Successful traders understand that having strategies for exiting is critical for attaining consistent success in the markets.

Broadly, here are the seven events that should motivate or help you to sell. These can be best described as:
1. Initial protective stops
2. Gaps against the prevailing trend
3. Price targets
4. Hard trailing stops
5. Trailing stops
6. Time stops
7. Moving average crossovers

Initial protective stops. In the interest of preservation of capital, this stop prompts your first decision to sell. Before thinking about how much money a trade will make, consider where you will exit if the trade does not go according to plan. By having a protective stop on a trade, you will not succumb to holding a position because you think "it is a good idea."

When initially entering the trade, the first technical consideration is the location and price levels of support and resistance. Make sure you are entering a position that is not too far extended from a decent level of support or resistance to set the protective stop. This initial stop ensures that if the stock does not act the way you expect, your account is not exposed to a catastrophic loss. For longs, stops should be placed just below the most recent support; for shorts, just above a recent resistance level. In other words, you are exploiting the definition of an uptrend (higher highs and higher lows in an uptrend and lower highs and lower lows in a downtrend) to remove the dangerous emotions that can enter the decision-making process.

Gaps against the prevailing trend. These dramatic gaps, normally more than five percent (versus more common gaps of one to two percent), occur when a stock in an uptrend suddenly gaps lower while you have a long position in the stock. Luckily, these gaps in trading, caused by an imbalance to the sell side while the stock is in a solid uptrend, are not all that common. When, however, we are caught in this predicament, it is often best to sell the *entire* position. A gap of this magnitude typically will not occur unless there is a serious fundamental development at the company, and because our entry may not have taken fundamentals into consideration, we are now in an unanticipated position. So, when in doubt, get out! Don't prolong the agony of a loser.

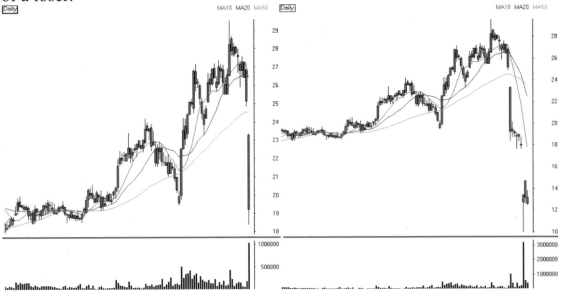

Figure 16.3 The chart on the left shows a stock which gapped lower and then continued lower for the rest of the day. The same stock is shown two weeks later on the right. RealTick by Townsend Analytics.

There is always a chance that the stock may bounce higher after you exit, but such moves typically will be short lived with a severely wounded stock. Think of a runner who falls into a roadside ditch during a marathon and breaks a leg. His competitive nature may push him to get up quickly and continue running, but when the adrenaline finally wears off, he will be left to deal with the excruciating pain of the fracture. Stocks which break severely from trend rarely recover fully, and it is best just to move on.

Price targets. It is a good idea to have a reasonable expectation about the point to which you believe a stock has the potential to rally. This gives you an estimated area where selling may occur. If your stock is in a solid uptrend that may be approaching a prior level of support, there is the potential for that past area of buying to offer resistance. A note of caution here – be careful to avoid selling *too much* of a stock that continues to have strong upward momentum because the biggest gains may still be ahead in this situation. Taking a little stock off the position reduces your overall risk, giving you a cushion in case the stock drops suddenly.

You also need to be cautious about taking target levels too literally as it is only a *theoretical* target based on your analysis. If a stock gives you a reason to sell before your target is hit, then forget the target and trade based on what the market is telling you. Don't be stubborn and give back profits waiting for that last $0.10/share. Bulls and bears make money, greedy pigs get slaughtered, and disciplined pigs get rich!

Hard trailing stops. These stops require the most skill, but by the time you get to this point, the stock is doing the work while your job is to monitor and adjust your risk levels as the stock moves higher. A hard trailing stop is based on the very definition of the trends from which you are attempting to extract money. As we know, the definition of an uptrend is "a series of higher highs and higher lows." This implies that breaking the series of higher lows is a violation of the trend, and that is a reason to sell. This stop takes some work because you have to cancel and replace orders. Nonetheless, this is fun because it means you are locking in profits.

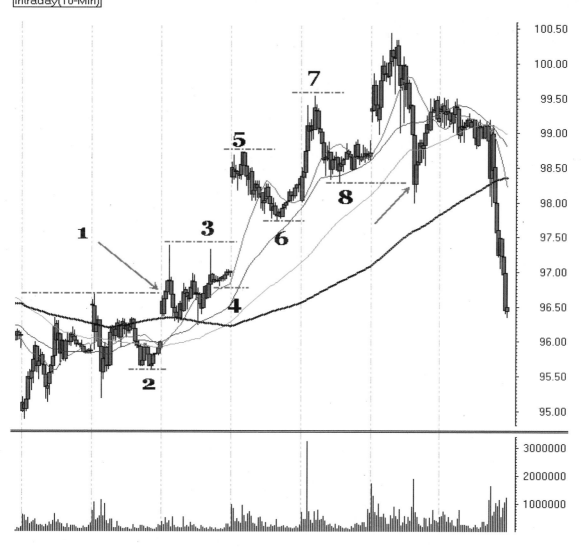

Figure 16.4 For a long trade, the trailing stop is raised to a level just below the higher low (even numbers) after the stock establishes new highs (odd numbers). For example, as the stock clears point 5, the stop is raised from point 4 to point 6. This process is repeated until the stock establishes a lower low (breaking below point 8). RealTick by Townsend Analytics

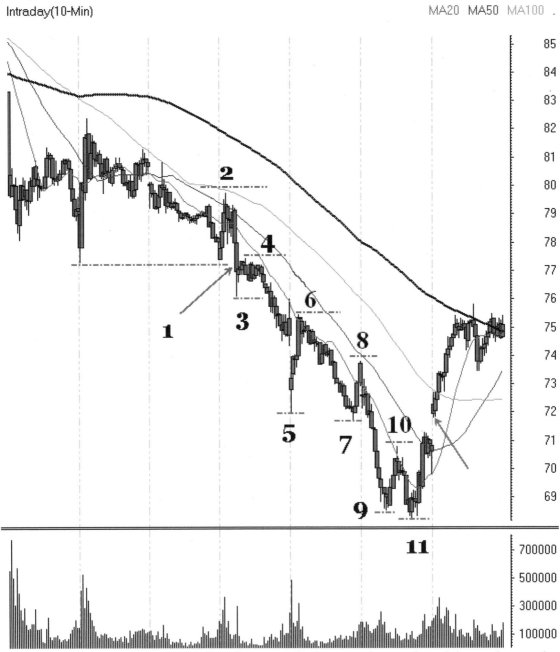

Figure 16.5 For a short trade, the stop is lowered to a level just above the lower highs (even numbers) after the stock establishes new lows (odd numbers). For example, as the stock establishes a new low by going below point 3, the stop should be lowered to point 4. This process is repeated until

the stock establishes a higher high (breaking above point 10). RealTick by Townsend Analytics

Trailing stops. This is my favorite stop to use on a day trade. This unique stop actually gives control of your order to the algorithm built into many trading platforms. The ideal situation in which to use a trailing stop is when you buy a stock that finds rapid upside velocity, pushing the stock quickly away from your hard stop. In a situation where the stock may run $1.00 or more in just a few minutes, you are faced with the dilemma of deciding whether to sell the position and lock in the gains or allow them to run further. We've all seen stocks that can run two to three dollars in the course of an hour or less, and we certainly don't want to allow a nice winner to turn into a loser. The emotions that can be dredged up from this experience tempt even the most disciplined traders to exit with the profit rather than allowing them to run further. Fortunately, technology has given us the opportunity to mitigate the emotional decision process with the trailing stop.

As the stock exhibits further strength, the trailing stop automatically gets adjusted higher, but it will never get adjusted lower. The trailing stop sets an actual stop – e.g., $0.15 (or whatever increment you choose) – below every new high the stock makes. Keep in mind that this will turn into a market order upon the stop being activated, and this can cause slippage in illiquid or fast moving markets.

Figure 16.6 This one-minute chart of MACR should be referenced with the order book in Figure 16.7 below. RealTick by Townsend Analytics.

Time	Order Details	Status	Time	Order Details	Status
9:52	Bought 500 MACR at 27.000000 with PSE-LX-ETNTOA (or	Completed	9:52	ARCA Order Status: New stop 27.27	Completed
9:52	Buy 500 MACR at 27.00 Deleted	Killed (Order (	9:52	ARCA Order Status: New stop 27.28	Completed
9:52	Cancel order 0b06-000c-002e-00 sent to exchange	Sent	9:52	ARCA Order Status: New stop 27.29	Completed
9:52	Order 0b06-000c-002e-00 killed by the exchange for rea	Completed	9:52	ARCA Order Status: New stop 27.30	Completed
9:52	Buy 500 MACR at 27.05 on ARCA (400 traded @ 27.0500)	Executed	9:52	ARCA Order Status: New stop 27.31	Completed
9:52	Bought 100 MACR at 27.050000 with PSE-LX-ETNTOA (or	Completed	9:52	ARCA Order Status: New stop 27.33	Completed
9:52	Bought 100 MACR at 27.050000 with PSE-LX-ETNTOA (or	Completed	9:52	ARCA Order Status: New stop 27.35	Completed
9:52	Bought 100 MACR at 27.050000 with PSE-LX-ETNTOA (or	Completed	9:52	ARCA Order Status: New stop 27.36	Completed
9:52	Bought 100 MACR at 27.050000 with PSE-LX-ETNTOA (or	Completed	9:52	ARCA Order Status: New stop 27.37	Completed
9:52	Cancel order 0b06-000c-002f-00 sent to exchange	Sent	9:52	ARCA Order Status: New stop 27.38	Completed
9:52	Order 0b06-000c-002f-00 killed by the exchange for reas	Completed	9:52	ARCA Order Status: New stop 27.39	Completed
9:52	Sell 900 MACR at Trailing Stop: .15 on ARCA (900 traded @	Executed	9:52	ARCA Order Status: New stop 27.40	Completed
9:52	ARCA Order Status: Pending trailing stop (trail=.15)	Completed	9:52	ARCA Order Status: New stop 27.41	Completed
9:52	ARCA Order Status: New stop 26.99	Completed	9:52	ARCA Order Status: New stop 27.44	Completed
9:52	ARCA Order Status: New stop 27.00	Completed	9:52	ARCA Order Status: New stop 27.45	Completed
9:52	ARCA Order Status: New stop 27.01	Completed	9:52	ARCA Order Status: New stop 27.46	Completed
9:52	ARCA Order Status: New stop 27.02	Completed	9:52	ARCA Order Status: New stop 27.47	Completed
9:52	ARCA Order Status: New stop 27.03	Completed	9:52	ARCA Order Status: New stop 27.48	Completed
9:52	ARCA Order Status: New stop 27.05	Completed	9:52	ARCA Order Status: New stop 27.50	Completed
9:52	ARCA Order Status: New stop 27.06	Completed	9:52	ARCA Order Status: New stop 27.51	Completed
9:52	ARCA Order Status: New stop 27.07	Completed	9:52	ARCA Order Status: New stop 27.53	Completed
9:52	ARCA Order Status: New stop 27.08	Completed	9:52	ARCA Order Status: New stop 27.54	Completed
9:52	ARCA Order Status: New stop 27.09	Completed	9:52	ARCA Order Status: New stop 27.55	Completed
9:52	ARCA Order Status: New stop 27.10	Completed	9:52	ARCA Order Status: New stop 27.56	Completed
9:52	ARCA Order Status: New stop 27.11	Completed	9:52	ARCA Order Status: New stop 27.58	Completed
9:52	ARCA Order Status: New stop 27.12	Completed	9:52	ARCA Order Status: New stop 27.60	Completed
9:52	ARCA Order Status: New stop 27.13	Completed	9:52	ARCA Order Status: New stop 27.61	Completed
9:52	ARCA Order Status: New stop 27.15	Completed	9:52	ARCA Order Status: New stop 27.62	Completed
9:52	ARCA Order Status: New stop 27.16	Completed	9:52	ARCA Order Status: New stop 27.63	Completed
9:52	ARCA Order Status: New stop 27.17	Completed	9:52	ARCA Order Status: New stop 27.65	Completed
9:52	ARCA Order Status: New stop 27.18	Completed	9:52	ARCA Order Status: New stop 27.66	Completed
9:52	ARCA Order Status: New stop 27.19	Completed	9:52	ARCA Order Status: New stop 27.67	Completed
9:52	ARCA Order Status: New stop 27.20	Completed	9:52	ARCA Order Status: New stop 27.68	Completed
9:52	ARCA Order Status: New stop 27.21	Completed	9:52	ARCA Order Status: New stop 27.69	Completed
9:52	ARCA Order Status: New stop 27.22	Completed	9:52	ARCA Order Status: New stop 27.70	Completed
9:52	ARCA Order Status: New stop 27.23	Completed	9:52	ARCA Order Status: New stop 27.71	Completed
9:52	ARCA Order Status: New stop 27.25	Completed	9:52	ARCA Order Status: New stop 27.73	Completed
9:52	ARCA Order Status: New stop 27.26	Completed	9:52	ARCA Order Status: New stop 27.74	Completed
9:52	ARCA Order Status: New stop 27.27	Completed	9:59	Sold 100 MACR at 27.710000 with PSE-LX-ETNTOA (orde	Completed
			9:59	Sold 800 MACR at 27.650000 with PSE-LX-ETNTOA (orde	Completed

Figure 16.7 This order book shows the purchase and sale of 900 shares of MACR. The stock was purchased with limit orders at 27.00 and 27.05. Almost as soon as the stock was purchased I placed a trailing stop of $0.15. You can see that the stop was adjusted over fifty times as the stock surged higher. After just seven minutes, the stop was triggered at 27.74 and was then executed at prices of 27.71 and 27.65. Trailing stops become market orders when they are activated and it often results in slippage.

The most difficult decision for a trailing stop is how much room to allow the stock to have. Fishermen can relate to this. If you have a big fish on the line and tighten the line too much, the fish is sure to break off and you never get the chance to taste your reward. Likewise, if you set the stop too tight, you can get shaken out of the position before the stock runs its course. How much room I give a trailing stop depends in great part on historical volatility and the price of the stock. The more volatile and higher-priced stocks need to be given extra room to wiggle, while less-volatile and lower-priced issues can usually be kept on a tight leash with just a $0.10-0.15 stop.

Time stops. These stops address the other form of market risk – time – and provide a way of exiting a position that is stagnant. If you haven't noticed this, you soon will – time can be a quiet killer of your equity. How many times have you neglected a stock in your account because it wasn't doing anything? The general guidelines that I use as time stops for day trades is 15 to 30 minutes, with more emphasis on the 30-minute level if the overall market is moving in the direction anticipated for the stock. For a swing trade, I typically give the stock two to three hours to get moving before I consider selling the position out near my cost basis. For position trades, my patience gets stretched easily, and I give the stock no more than one to two days to get moving before I start to think my timing is off. When I get stopped out because of time, I will often re-enter the stock if it exhibits signs that it may be ready to move later on.

Moving average crossovers. These often signal the end of a prevailing trend and present a good time to take profits on a position. Moving averages are simple technical indicators, but are often misunderstood. In essence, a moving average crossover represents a lack of consensus about whether buyers or sellers are in control. Recognition of a crossover signals that the stock may need time to digest the gains, and as a trend follower there should be no clearer sign that it is time to exit gracefully with your accumulated profits before the market relieves you of them.

The most logical approach to exiting your position is to objectively listen to the message of the market and take action based on the message as it reveals itself. I am partial to using a combination of the strategies laid out. I like to establish a large position when I perceive low risk, but at the first signs of momentum I almost always scale out of the trade with a sell that will cover the transaction costs. I will typically exit the remainder of the position by utilizing one or more of the strategies laid out in this chapter.

CHAPTER 17
TRADING TIPS AND TRUISMS TO THINK ABOUT

Anyone who's been involved in trading or investing in the markets over an extended period of time and has a passion for the experience learns lessons along the way. While a few come from discussions with other traders and general book/seminar learning, *by far* most are learned in the school of hard knocks – the wallet, the disappointment, and self-doubt. Yes, of course, there are joys along the way, but during the learning period, you get kicked in the butt a great deal. So, the lessons I've learned best over the years have come from adversity. I've learned to temper the tough ones with some general understandings, which are now closer to the bone than they once were.

Many, if not most, traders and investors come into the market with a preconceived notion of what to expect. It's just buying low and selling high, right? How hard can that be? But along the way, emotions creep in, and if you've read this book, you'll now know how easy it is to be one of the sheep versus one of the wolves.

Originally, I jotted down all the important lessons that reside in my head -- and there are probably more that mirror these – but then decided to organize them into rough categories. What I found was instructive. More than one-third of them related to emotions and discipline, and there were crossovers of emotion and discipline in other categories, as well. If that tells you how much of an ongoing kaleidoscope of study the markets are and what a head game they become, then good. I have done my job.

PRICE:
In the markets, price is the only thing that really matters. Only price pays!

Don't chase price, and as important as volume is, don't wait for it to make your decisions. All decisions to buy or sell should be predetermined and based on price, because price action rules all!

Don't waste time arguing your views about a stock or the market. Let the market decide. Price is the final arbiter, and the market will determine who is right.

Argue with price at your own peril, the market will always win.

ABOUT THE MARKETS:
The market is a leading indicator of the economy. Economists would be the best traders if a strong understanding of the economy was necessary to trade successfully.

The most difficult job on Wall Street is picking tops and bottoms.

Bull markets foster bad habits amongst traders, and bear markets bring about a remembrance and respect for risk.

Do not force your opinion on the markets. The market doesn't care what you or I think should happen. Trade what you see, not what you think.

There are no sure things and everyone gets what they deserve from the markets. Be prepared for all potential outcomes, and never underestimate the presence of risk.

From false moves come fast moves, and the second mouse gets the cheese.

The unexpected happens often, and markets do not always act rationally. Always plan for the worst. If you are aware of all potential scenarios, you can make calm, rational decisions in any market environment.

MONEY:
No one is bigger than the market, and no one is immune from the potential of financial ruin. Big money doesn't always mean smart money.

"Smart money" doesn't always do smart things with their money.

Profitable trades which allow you to recover from losses feel great, but never as good as fresh profits do.

Risk management and position sizing are more important than what you choose to trade.

Trade smaller share size when you experience a losing streak or during periods of heightened market uncertainty.

Trading size should be looked at as more of a function of experience, a respect for the omnipresent risk and depth of market knowledge than the financial resources available to trade with.

Understand the presence of and continually reassess risks. Your most important job is that of risk manager.

Don't get caught up in meeting daily, weekly or monthly goals for a certain percentage or dollar amount. Focus on what you can control and how well you handle varying market conditions.

Positions that are entered correctly will tend to move quickly in your favor.

EMOTIONS:

No one is immune from the emotions of greed and fear. Leveraging your capital will also leverage these emotions, which increases risks.

Monitor your emotions and decision-making as closely as you observe price action. Do not allow your emotions to influence your buy-and-sell decisions.

It is always the "dumb mistake" that you "knew not to do" that hurts you most. Never let your guard down since emotions and complacency are the enemies.

Never trade out of frustration. The market punishes angry traders.

Cash is a position. You don't always have to be engaged. Cash allows for objective analysis when others fall victim to emotional decisions. (It is better to be on the sidelines wishing you were in the market than it is to be in the market wishing you were out).

Complacency is the silent killer of equity.

Don't be stubborn and hold losing positions. Your ego will heal from taking a small loss much quicker than your equity will recover from large draw downs.

Trade only when you have a proper mindset. If you are tired, hung over, or experiencing an emotional time in your life, judgment can be clouded and you will not trade well.

Be flexible in your opinion and be prepared to be wrong.

DISCIPLINE:

Discipline and patience are your friends; emotions are the enemy.

Discipline helps control problems stemming from ego and complacency.

Bulls and bears make money, greedy pigs get slaughtered, and disciplined pigs get rich.

Anticipate all market possibilities, and be disciplined enough to participate only when price action confirms your theories.

In order to plan your trade and trade your plan, you need to be a good analyst *and* a good trader.

Only initiate a trade when there is a perceived edge; then implement your plan with discipline.

Have the discipline to exit at the first signs of trouble. Being wrong at times is inevitable, but staying wrong is stupid.

Be disciplined to keep learning. Never believe you have it all figured out.

Defense wins this game! Think survival and add discipline to your plan first; one loser left unchecked can ruin you.

NEWS AND ADVICE:

More information is not necessarily better. News can cloud your judgment and lead you to believe the market is wrong, not you.

Focus on what is going to help you make money today, not on knowing trivial facts and statistics about a company.

Rely upon yourself only. There are many excellent newsletters and advisory services; find one or two that match your approach, but then make each idea your own.

Do not talk about your trading positions, and don't trust others who talk about theirs. Always verify information you hear with objective analysis of price action.

If you need other people's advice about a position, you probably should have exited it already.

News comes out at short-term turning points and often *confirms* the existing trend to the fundamental crowd.

INSIDE THE MARKET/TRENDS, AND OTHER MISCELLANY:
Volume and volatility are greatest near turning points and lessen with trend development.

When stocks don't do what they are expected, a violent move in the opposite direction often occurs as more participants are trapped with losing positions.

Cover partial shorts into panic selloffs and sell partial longs into euphoric rises. It is a good idea to liquidate partial positions when the stock responds to news. Exit positions when you can, not when you have to.

If it is hard to buy, it is going higher. If it is hard to sell, it is going lower.

Lose your opinion, not your capital. The market is not always rational and "reasons" are often revealed *after* price has moved.

By entering your long and short positions at the onset of short-term momentum, you have a greater chance of being ahead of the crowd and thereby mitigate the risk of time.

Heightened times of overall market uncertainty can be compensated for with analysis on shorter timeframes and smaller trading size.

Keep an eye on the more speculative stocks to measure the mood of the "fast money," as their actions tend to lead the overall market. When speculative money becomes less aggressive and momentum names start to decline quickly, it is time to become more defensive.

When in doubt, stay out, switch to shorter timeframe for clarity, or find something else to trade.

Most people make their market analysis much more difficult than it needs to be. Keep your analysis simple by staying focused on market structure.

Only your opinion matters to your positions, so do your own analysis and research before you commit your capital.

A mediocre trade setup in the hands of a good trader is more valuable than an excellent setup in the hands of a mediocre trader.

Anticipate all potential scenarios, but wait for price confirmation before taking action to buy or sell.

Tell your friends to buy this book.

CHAPTER 18
PUTTING IT ALL TOGETHER

With a firm understanding of market structure and how stocks are "supposed to" trade now under your belt, how do you then put that knowledge to use to achieve consistent profits in the market? As emphasized throughout this book, emotions are the enemy in trading and need to be minimized as much as possible in the decision-making process. One technique that lessens those emotions is to initiate your search for trading ideas outside of market hours when the constant flow of changing price information has been temporarily turned off until the next session. It is important to have a methodical approach when you scour the market for new trading ideas.

Here's how I do it. My hunt for the best stocks to trade on Monday begins on Friday afternoon or early Saturday morning when I make additions and deletions to my "master" list of stocks. The end of a work week, when trading action is still fresh in your mind, allows you to keep in tune with the markets and use some logical intuition in finding trading candidates. The master list is one which includes 300 to 400 symbols of stocks' with solid trends, unusual volume, market-leading stocks and ETFs. I look through each stock on the master list and narrow the list to between 100 to 150 stocks that will be my "week scan" list. The week scan list is comprised of the stocks I believe will provide the best trading candidates for the next week, typically those that have entered a new trending campaign on a daily timeframe. I also pay careful attention to trending stocks that appear to be experiencing a pullback that could refresh back into alignment with the primary trend over the course of the next week.

I am not necessarily looking specifically for long or short opportunities, just opportunities, period. If there is momentum on either side of the market, I want to identify it so I have a go-to list of ideas for a bullish or bearish trading environment. I am always aware of the overall technical condition of the market, and everything must be anticipated so there are no surprises if the market decides to reverse course the following week.

While I do not exclude a stock based solely on price, I personally tend to trade stocks priced from $5 to $40/share most effectively, so I like to see those stocks show up on my searches. I also recognize from previous trading results that I am not very good at trading stocks that are tied to natural resources, so I will be more stringent in adding any commodity-related issues.

Most of the stocks I trade are NASDAQ issues, but as the NYSE trading floor transitions to an electronic environment, I find myself trading listed stocks more frequently, which opens up more good opportunities. I also tend to trade well in stocks with an average daily volume ranging between 400,000 and five million shares per day because they are liquid enough to get into and out of without too much difficulty.

Note, however, that the above is what works best *for me*. You need to find those stocks that work best for *you*.

At Market Close
Each day after the market closes, I search my weekly scan list for potential stocks to trade the next day. For stock setups that may trigger a buy or sell on a Tuesday, this hunt begins on Monday afternoon within 15 to 30 minutes of the market close. If I wait too long, I lose some of the feel from that trading day. I also want to have uninterrupted time away from the market for the rest of the evening.

The end of an active trading day can leave me mentally exhausted, so I get up and stretch, get a snack or, on occasion, work out before beginning the search for trading candidates. Whatever you do to relax and switch from the trader mentality to that of an analyst will help you be more objective in your search.

I do not look through my "master list" of stocks each day (too long of a list), but do view all of the unusual moves with at least one million shares occurring on that day once the market has closed. I pay a great deal more attention to the stocks on the percentage-gainer list than loser because I trade them better, but if you like to trade the short side, the percentage-loser list often contains many stocks that will continue lower for several days. When I find a stock which looks like it may be at the beginning of a several-day move, I add it to the "week scan" list that was compiled prior to Monday morning.

Once I am in the proper frame of mind, I view each of the 100 to 150 stocks on my "week scan" list. I place a daily chart on one monitor and a 30-minute timeframe on another. I can set my market minder so that when I click on a symbol, it will populate these two charts simultaneously. Then I can use the down arrow on the keyboard to change the symbol quickly. On the first pass-through of this list, I pay most attention to the 30-minute timeframe, but I am fully aware of the longer-term trend on the daily timeframe on the other monitor. When I see a stock that interests me on the 30-minute timeframe, I jot down the symbol on a sheet of paper and repeat the process until I have combed through the entire list.

I now have a new shorter list of stocks, about 20 to 40 symbols (my "day scan" list), which I cull to just a handful of stocks that appear to be near a low-risk, high-potential trade entry level. At this point, I pay closer attention to the 10-minute timeframe and note volume trends, proximity of support or resistance levels and possible trigger points for a trade. If a stock appears to have a high probability of directional movement, I try to discern which key level will need to be broken for a low-risk tradable momentum move to develop. If the focus stock is in a daily Stage 2 and a Stage 1 on the 10-minute timeframe, I try to identify the point where the trends will be aligned. If, for instance, the uptrending stock has found support over the last day or two and has formed short-term resistance at 24.50, I will then write 24.48 next to the symbol. This level will then be entered into my trading platform's alerts section. If the stock trades at that level during the following day, I will be alerted both audibly and visually. It is important to set the alert a couple of pennies below the actual level at which more important buying will be triggered; it gives me the chance to pull the stock up on a live chart and on a level two screen for more active monitoring and last-minute planning before tripping the trigger on a trade.

By being in a position to watch a stock as the momentum builds below a key level, I am able to *anticipate* movement rather than reacting to something which has already moved. Being a predatory anticipator allows me to minimize the likelihood of allowing emotion to cloud my short-term thinking when the stock signals an alert.

Once I go through the entire list of stocks and set my alerts, I do a quick, but thorough, review of the markets, writing down my thoughts about the likelihood of movement for the next day as well as key levels of support and resistance in the process. I will often enter some of these market levels in the alerts so I am not caught off guard by any unexpected macro market movement if my attention is focused on individual stocks. Once I have completed these rituals, my work is done for the evening.

The Pre-market

I usually sit down at the trading desk about one hour before the market opens. The first thing I do is to check for any pre-market movement in stocks that I may have held overnight. If a stock position moves against me by more than two to three percent, I will monitor the stock closely in the pre-market to make sure it doesn't cause further damage to my equity. If the weakness persists, I typically exit the trade quickly, particularly if there is heavy volume and it looks like the stock will continue to move against me in the regular session. Dealing with losing positions in overnight trades immediately keeps me from obsessing over every transaction in the stock, instead focusing on a more productive setup with better opportunity to make back those initial losses.

If an overnight position gaps in my favor I typically exit at least a portion of the stock in the pre-market to lock in a small gain. The pre-market exits do not come about randomly, however. I monitor a tick chart (varying the amount of ticks depending on the level of trading activity in the stock, sometimes using 50 ticks for stocks with low volume or as many as 500 for very actively traded stocks) with a VWAP moving average and remain in the position as long as the VWAP is moving in the direction of my trade. Once the stock moves below (assuming a long position) the VWAP in the pre-market, I exit the majority of my position and then maintain the balance in hopes of attaining a more favorable exit during regular market hours.

If there is no action in the pre-market affecting my trades, my next step is to check to see how overnight trading in the futures markets is likely to influence the day and make any necessary adjustments to my market alert levels. I then review all of the stocks in my day watch list to see if any unusual pre-market activity exists. If a long candidate is gapping lower by more than two percent or so, I eliminate it from consideration, just as I will eliminate a down trending stock that is gapping higher by about two percent. If pre-market volume or price movement exists in the stocks on my watch list, I am careful not to allow myself to get excited and initiate a new position during this session. Pre-market trading activity is often very thin and choppy and is generally better used to liquidate overnight holds than to initiate new positions.

Once I have completed a run through of the stocks on my list, I read through news headlines to see if there is anything that may affect the trading in the stocks I am considering that day. This process usually takes about 5 minutes. I rarely read a full news story about a stock since I rely on the market's interpretation of the news for my buy and sell decisions.

My pre-market ritual cements my thoughts about the most likely scenario for the overall market that day, and gives me a bias toward either long or short trading opportunities. I try to anticipate whether the market is most likely to continue the most recent directional movement, consolidate the recent movement or reverse the short-term trend.

In actuality, the most likely scenario for the market each day is that it will consolidate within a range. As discussed earlier in the trend section, markets tend to thrust and consolidate. Because directional moves typically occur in short bursts of activity, most of the time they are consolidating those moves. If the major market averages are in a primary trend higher, I tend to focus most of my attention on long opportunities just as I will focus most of my attention on short opportunities when the overall trend is lower. When the markets are showing longer-term consolidating action I try not to have a directional bias beyond the trend of individual stocks. The good thing about a neutral market environment is that there are often excellent opportunities to be found on the long and short sides of the market. Of course, this is just what I consider to be the most likely scenario; the market may completely disagree with my assessment, so I must remain flexible in my opinion. Having long and short trade candidates on my list assures I will be prepared for volatility in either direction.

Market	Strong Stock	Weak Stock
Unchanged	even to up 2%	even to down 2%
Up 2%	up 2 to 5%	even to +2%
Down 2%	even to down 2%	down 2 to 5%

Figure 18.1 The trends of the overall market will play a major factor in how individual stocks trade. Though not the result of any formal study, this table is a rough approximation of the concept of relative strength.

With just five to ten minutes before the opening bell, I make another check of the charts for stocks on my daily list to make final notes or adjustments to my alert levels. This is the time for me to finalize the two or three stocks on which to concentrate most intently at the open. Finally, I will run to the bathroom, top off my coffee and get ready for the action.

At the Open

With the initial flurry of trading activity at the open of the market, it is important to take a deep breath and relax. This is the most nerve-wracking time of day. It is easy to get caught up in making emotional decisions at the open, making regrettable buys or sells. Having a plan of action allows you to be objective when others are often making impulsive decisions. The initial market action is fast and furious; it is common for ten or more alerts to be triggered in the opening moments. Obviously, you cannot and most likely should not, take trades in all of those stocks. My focus will be on a 5-minute or 2-minute chart, and I will be paying the most attention to the stocks I think are the highest-probability candidates — those marked on the notes in front of me.

I try to focus on the one or two that are trading in the direction of the trend of the overall market at that point in the day. I do not have a hard and fast rule as to how long I wait before deciding to buy or sell. Some days it will be right away, and on other days it may take an hour before I see something worthy of a trade. This is where trading experience pays off. I am always particularly cautious during the first 30 or so minutes of trading because it is the time when the buyers and sellers are fighting the fiercest battles for control of the daily trend. Reversals can come quickly and do severe financial damage if you aren't disciplined about exiting a loser unemotionally. How long you wait to buy or sell depends a great deal on variables for the day. Ask a surgeon how deep to make an incision, and he/she will tell you that it depends on the type of surgery, the age and physical condition of the patient, etc. In the market, it depends on the overall market trend, volume of the initial move, if critical news is due to be released, and numerous other factors.

If you have done the proper work outside of market hours, observing price action becomes more objective and allows you to keep your cool during the chaotic open of trading each day.

The Trading Day

As the trading day progresses, it is essential to have a routine for filtering through the list of trade candidates you established prior to the start of the day. After I have placed initial trades – and maybe even taken some profits

– I try to look through my daily list of stocks to hone in on developing opportunities. I typically look at the 5-minute chart for this analysis to see if any stocks are approaching what appear to be key levels. If I uncover any candidates, I drill down to a 2-minute chart to get a better idea of where to reset my alarm or, if it is ready, where to make my entry and how much risk I am willing to accept. I typically run through this list several times during the day, searching for unfolding activity that could be profitable.

Note that the risk/reward ratio you calculated in your analysis the prior evening will change as the trading activity unfolds. This may render some of the setups invalid or too risky to consider, so wait until they develop further and offer a lower-risk entry. Your trading plan needs to have a degree of flexibility. This doesn't mean that you should be willing to go short a stock you thought was a good long candidate or vice versa, but that you need to adjust to the constantly changing market activity. *Come into the market each day prepared for any type of environment, not just the one that suits your bias from the prior day's analysis.* Please note that the shorter term your trading focus is, the greater your need to be able to unemotionally and accurately read the live auction process presented to you.

Once the market has quieted down to the point where I am compulsively checking through the lists, I conduct other market research. This intraday research is not an attempt to find new ideas; rather it gauges overall market psychology. I do this by reading news headlines and occasionally a full story from major online business portals and some high-quality blogs. Be careful not to put too much weight in the opinions of a blogger, though, as the ease of creating a blog does not assure that the author has any real trading experience. See www.alphatrends.net for a current list of blogs which I read on a regular basis.

I don't find all of my ideas based on my original research. Sometimes I will read about an interesting company on another website or see a news story that makes me want to investigate a stock further. I may see a research report on a stock that piques my interest, but will *never* commit any money on a trade based solely on what someone else tells me. I *always* check the trading action on multiple timeframes before I commit a single penny. There is nothing wrong with using advisory services or listening to the opinions of other traders you respect, but it is your money at risk and you alone are responsible for what you decide to buy or sell.

On days when the market activity is very slow and I do not perceive an edge, I can take a midday nap, go for a bike ride, take a run or do something other than stare at my screen obsessively looking for something to trade. This freedom is the part of being a trader I enjoy so much. When I do return to my desk, I feel reinvigorated and can concentrate better.

The Pre-Close
The final hour of trading can be a busy time, particularly on a day when there is a strong market directional trend bias. There can be some excellent stock moves in the last hour, which present opportunities you may have missed in the morning. Aside from continuing to trade, the final hour is when decisions need to be made about whether or not stock positions should be held overnight. If you have researched the stock and are comfortable that there are no known potential catalysts that may disrupt the stock trend, there is no reason that winners should not be allowed to run the next day.

Quite often I sell a portion of my winners before the close, which not only allows me to book some profits, but also reduce my overnight market exposure and, thus, my overall risk (more defensive maneuvering). If I find myself in a losing position near the end of the day, I almost always sell it out so I can end my day with the comfort of not being burdened by a losing position. I will likely be able to re-enter the position the next day, perhaps at an even more favorable price.

Performance Anxiety
There is a tendency for traders to feel bad about underperforming the market averages on a daily or weekly basis, but success as a trader does not come from such short-term measurements or comparisons. We all have our cycles of under- or out-performance, but over time the true measurement of success in trading is being consistently profitable regardless of how the overall market is performing.

At the end of each trading day you shouldn't focus solely on your P/L. Instead, focus on your thought process during the day and how well you executed your plan. If you consistently execute your trades according to plan and still lose money, then you need to reevaluate your approach. While there is definitely a cyclical rhythm to the market, no strategy will always work. You need to constantly and objectively review what is working and what is not so you can make necessary adjustments to your plan.

Very important to your trading success is the ability and introspection to ask yourself whether your results are attributable to your ability to see the markets clearly and execute your plan with discipline, or if the market is making it easy to book profitable trades. There are times when the market makes a trader's job much easier, and huge profits accrue over short periods of time. Unfortunately, those times do not last. The trick is to hold onto those profits when the market becomes more difficult. Many traders experience large losses after a string of profitable trades because they succumb to the feeling that "the losses aren't real; they are just giving back profits." This dangerous thinking is borne from complacency as a result of a feeling of infallibility that then leaves the trader vulnerable to large losses. *Always take losses seriously, and minimize them at your first opportunity – without hesitation.* Doing otherwise is the mark of an amateur who makes big money in a bull market, gives it all back when the trend ends and then blames their losses on the market. Professionals listen objectively to the message of the markets and adapt quickly to changing market conditions.

Things to Consider
Before entering a trade on any timeframe, there are certain technical factors that should be considered. Varying market conditions make it impossible for any list to include all factors which should be considered. The first consideration to be made is the existence of a high-probability trade with defined and limited risk relative to the potential reward. The existence of these criteria allow you to have an edge in your trade, and without an edge, you are gambling.

To define your edge in trading you need to:
- Trade in the direction of the primary trend (identified by the direction of the 50-day moving average).
- Initiate long trades only where the moving averages have a positive slope.
- Initiate short sales only where the moving averages have a negative slope.
- Be aware of overall market trends as well as key support and resistance levels, while not ignoring a strong stock setup because of an unfavorable market backdrop (you may want to adjust your trade size based on overall market conditions, as well).
- Time your entries on shorter-term timeframes as the trends come into alignment with the larger trends.

- Define your risk based on market action (support and resistance levels) rather than on percentages or other random methods. Stops on long positions should be placed just under the most recent higher low. Stops on shorts should be placed just above the most recent lower high.
- Identify likely support and resistance levels to determine where a trend may lose momentum (the basis of identifying potential price objectives).
- Know that large short positions represent future demand but short sellers are often right; their timing may just be off.
- Understand what potential catalysts may exist to increase trading activity. Being aware of the timing of fundamental reports does not require you to be an expert in the business of the company.
- Enter at the onset of a new short-term momentum campaign. For longs, buy as the stock breaks out past short-term levels of resistance. Short entries should be initiated as short-term levels of ssupport are broken.
- Cut losses as soon as your stop levels are violated.
- Study volume patterns to determine the likelihood of trend continuation. Unusual trading volume is a reason to watch the stock more closely.
- Exit partial positions when stocks move suddenly in your favor; don't look a gift horse in the mouth.
- Trade management should occur on the shorter-term timeframe and should be based on the definition of trend.
- Manage your winners with patience, and exit as the trend shows signs of reversal.

Consideration of these factors and entering trades when there is a preponderance of technical evidence which supports a move in the anticipated direction should lead to more profitable trade setups. Of course, there are no riskless directional trades, which is why no trade plan is complete without a backup plan.

Plan

To succeed in the markets you need to listen objectively to its' message, place reasonably sized trades relative to account size and then manage risk. You need to possess a deep understanding of the way the markets work to obtain that objectivity. Market mastery begins with understanding the cyclical flow of capital and understanding how the components of the market come together to provide a recognizable structure.

In theory, trading is simple – buy low and sell high. It is easy to confuse simple-to-understand concepts with difficult-to-implement strategies. If you have seen Tiger Woods play golf, Michael Phelps swim the butterfly for 200 meters or Tom Brady throw the football 50 yards down field directly into the arms of a receiver, it looks easy. To a newer market participant, so does trading. The fact is that while it may be easy to "see the plays," only the players with the most practice and experience will be able to consistently implement those plays. The average sports fan will not be able to compete with world-class athletes. However, most want-to-be traders look at trading with the professionals in a different light, figuring that all they need is money to compete. However, the principles are much the same – most well-capitalized amateurs in the markets will give their money to savvy market participants who possess more market knowledge and experience.

A bad idea in the hands of a good trader is generally going to provide a better result than a good idea in the hands of a trader with less-developed skills. It is much easier to be a good stock picker than it is to be a good trader, so until you develop your trading skills, share size should be kept small relative to account balances. When you have the proper trading experience and understand trading dynamics as well as market structure, you are in an enviable position.

There is no single formula for success in the stock market, no matter which timeframe you employ. If you are looking for an easy money-making scheme by trading stocks, you are wasting your time. The only way to succeed is to work hard, be disciplined and commit to learning as much as possible. Technical analysis is a tool that allows you to be totally objective in your studies of the market and, at a glance, visualize the only true constant in the ever-changing market -- human nature.

As humans we tend to act or react to a set of circumstances in very predictable ways. If we can understand what others are experiencing emotionally, we can often position ourselves to take advantage of their weaknesses (I never said the market is a "nice" place).

Trading is about making money. Be like the most successful participants, and learn to look at the market with a cold and indifferent eye, only striking when the odds are truly in your favor. Focus on growing and learning from human nature and become a lifelong student of the markets, and you will achieve your goals.

About the Author

Brian Shannon is an experienced and successful trader, speaker and educator. Involved full time in the markets since 1991, he has worked as a broker, owned a day trading firm, managed a hedge fund, ran a proprietary trading desk while simultaneously being the most profitable trader of that prop firm. As Head of Research and Training for MarketWise, Brian taught thousands of trader's world-wide.

Brian's work has been published or written about in Technical Analysis of Stocks & Commodities, Barron's, Active Trader, Stock Futures and Options Magazine, and hundreds of online sites.

Brian is best known for his daily technical analysis videos on www.alphatrends.net and www.wallstrip.com

**View free technical analysis videos from Brian at
www.alphatrends.net**